# LIVERPOOL
## PLAYER BY PLAYER

# IVAN PONTING

# ACKNOWLEDGEMENTS

The author would like to thank the following: Pat and Rosie Ponting; Steve Small; all at Colorsport; Ian Callaghan; Arthur Fenna; Graham Hart; John Hudson; Roger Hunt; David Johnson; Brian Jones; Alan Kennedy; Billy Liddell; Gary Talbot; Tom Bailey; Moira Banks; Josh Barrett; Chris and Jo Forster; Nick Gibbs; George Herringshaw; Nick Humpage.

The author is also grateful for permission to reproduce photographs. The majority are from Colorsport, with a large contribution from Associated Sports Photography. There are also pictures from Steve Hale, Stewart Kendall, Gary Talbot and LP Sports Service.

Efforts have been made to trace copyright holders of all photographs used in this book. We apologise for any omissions, which are unintentional, and would be pleased to include appropriate acknowledgement in any subsequent edition.

Pictured on the front cover are: Ian Rush *(centre)* and *(clockwise from top left)* Kenny Dalglish, Roger Hunt, John Barnes, Ian Callaghan and Billy Liddell. On the back are Bill Shankly *(centre)* and *(clockwise from top left)* Graeme Souness, Kevin Keegan, Ron Yeats, Peter Beardsley, Terry McDermott, Alan Hansen, Tommy Smith and Ray Clemence.

First published in 1990 by
THE CROWOOD PRESS
Ramsbury, Marlborough
Wiltshire SN8 2HE

Text copyright © 1990 by Ivan Ponting
Design: Steve Small
Illustrations copyright © 1990 as credited

British Library Cataloguing in Publication Data
Ponting, Ivan
Liverpool: player by player.
I. England. Association football. Clubs. Liverpool Football Club.
Players, to 1990
I. Title
**796.334630922**

ISBN 1-85223-526-8

Printed by BAS Printers Limited,
Over Wallop, Hampshire

# INTRODUCTION

Footballers make splendid heroes, and in recent years none have been more acclaimed than the men of Anfield. The story of Liverpool FC has been told many times, but never before, I believe, has there been a detailed look at each player, since the dawn of the Shankly era, to wear the red shirt. This book is an attempt, by a lifelong soccer addict, to fill that gap.

To that end, I have collected a photograph of every man to represent the Reds in the Football League, FA Cup, League Cup (under all its banners) and European competition since December 1959. Alongside each picture is the player's career record and, in almost every case, my personal assessment of his footballing attributes and position in the history of the club. Where an individual has played in so few games as to render such coverage meaningless, the figures stand alone. All records are complete until the end of the 1989/90 League season.

My intent has been to depict, in words, the essence of each player, and to conjure up an impression of his style on the field. Thus, only the basic statistics – games played, goals scored, previous clubs etc – are included. Liverpool appearance and scoring figures refer to all matches (a breakdown for each competition appears in a separate section at the end of the book) but under the heading of 'Other Clubs', the games and goals are in the Football League only. The dates in large type refer to the seasons in which the player appeared in the Reds' first team, not when he joined or left the club. Under 'Honours' I have included only those won as a Liverpool player, except in the case of international caps, the figures for which cover each man's complete career to date. All transfer fees mentioned are those favoured in the press, as clubs do not usually issue official figures.

Though the main part of the book begins with the arrival of Bill Shankly, I have set the scene with a brief look at the earlier post-war years, in which the club's fluctuating fortunes included a League Championship, a trip to Wembley, relegation and a seemingly never-ending battle to get out of the Second Division. Then, in roughly chronological order, comes my portraits of the men who made Liverpool great. I hope I have managed to jog a few memories.

Ivan Ponting,
Chewton Mendip,
August 1990.

# CONTENTS

# BEFORE THE REVOLUTION

ALBERT STUBBINS

It's not easy to imagine it now, but Liverpool Football Club did exist before the Shankly revolution. Indeed, the first post-war season saw the Reds lift the League Championship, and in 1950 they reached Wembley, where they were beaten by Arsenal in the FA Cup Final. That side boasted fine individuals such as Billy Liddell, Albert Stubbins and Jack Balmer and was a credit to manager George Kay, who was to retire through ill health in 1951.

He was replaced by Don Welsh, who introduced new blood to the side, but it was not enough to stop a gradual slide which culminated in relegation in 1953/54. Despite narrowly missing out on promotion in 1955/56, Don was dismissed, and the job of putting Liverpool back among the elite was handed to the club's former skipper, Phil Taylor. He held the reins for three Second Division campaigns, finishing third, fourth and fourth again before bowing to the strain and stepping down in November 1959. Then came Shankly – and life at Anfield was never the same again.

Pictured on these two pages are the leading players in the years of mixed fortunes between 1946 and 1959. Turn over to begin meeting the men who, over the subsequent three decades, took part in the most remarkable success story in the history of English soccer.

## FA CUP FINALISTS 1949-50

Back row *(left to right):*

GEORGE KAY (manager)

PHIL TAYLOR (35/6-53/4, wing-half, 345 games, 34 goals).

RAY LAMBERT (45/6-55/6. full-back, 341 games, 2 goals).

CYRIL SIDLOW (46/7-50/1, goalkeeper, 165 games, 0 goals).

BOB PAISLEY (45/6-53/4, wing-half, 278 games, 13 goals).

EDDIE SPICER (45/6-53/4, full-back/wing-half, 168 games, 2 goals).

ALBERT SHELLEY (trainer)

Front row:

JIMMY PAYNE (48/9-55/6, winger, 245 games, 42 goals).

KEVIN BARON (45/6-53/4, inside-forward, 152 games, 33 goals).

CYRIL DONE (39/40-51/2, centre-forward, 109 games, 37 goals).

WILLIE FAGAN (37/8-51/2, forward, 185 games, 57 goals).

BILLY LIDDELL (45/6-60/1, forward, 537 games, 229 goals).

LAURIE HUGHES (45/6-57/8, centre-half, 326 games, 1 goal).

Top row *(left to right):*

BILL JONES (46/7-53/4, utility player, 278 games, 17 goals).

JOHN EVANS (53/4-56/7, inside-forward, 106 games, 53 goals).

ROY SAUNDERS (52/3-58/9, wing-half, 144 games, 1 goal).

Centre row *(left to right):*

GEOFF TWENTYMAN (53/4-59/60, left-half, 184 games, 19 goals).

BRIAN JACKSON (51/2-57/8, winger, 131 games, 12 goals).

BARRY WILKINSON (53/4-59/60, wing-half, 79 games, 0 goals).

Bottom row *(left to right):*

TOMMY YOUNGER (56/7-58/9, goalkeeper, 127 games, 0 goals).

LOUIS BIMPSON (52/3-59/60, centre-forward, 100 games, 40 goals).

DOUG RUDHAM (54/5-59/60, goalkeeper, 66 games, 0 goals).

Left:
JACK BALMER (35/6-51/2, inside-forward, 313 games, 111 goals).

Far left:
ALBERT STUBBINS (46/7-52/3, centre-forward, 180 games, 83 goals).

DON WELSH

PHIL TAYLOR

JACK BALMER

# BILLY LIDDELL

It is scarcely possible to exaggerate the stature of Billy Liddell in the history of Liverpool FC. As a footballer he thrilled the Anfield faithful; as a man he warmed their hearts; as a symbol of all that was fine in the field of sporting endeavour he was unmatchable.

For nearly 15 years the self-effacing Scottish winger cum centre-forward was the outstanding player for a club which experienced fleeting moments of glory but which, in general, was a frustrated hotbed of unfulfilled potential. Had he been born two, three or four decades later and played under Shankly or Paisley, Fagan or Dalglish, he would have been knee-deep in honours. As it was he had to be content with a solitary League Championship medal and the knowledge that not for nothing was the team he graced known as 'Liddellpool'.

Billy signed on at Anfield as a promising flankman in 1939 and then saw the first six years of his career lost to the war. During the conflict he served as an RAF navigator but his soccer talents were not entirely redundant. He played almost 150 times for his new club in emergency competitions and served notice that here was something special.

In January 1946, with life gradually returning to something approaching normality, he made his official Liverpool debut five days short of his 24th birthday, scoring at Chester in the FA Cup. But it was in the following campaign that Billy Liddell really set sail on the course that was to earn him sporting immortality on Merseyside.

Playing 35 games as the Reds took the title, he revealed the pace and power which were to become his hallmarks. Billy was particularly dangerous running at defenders and cutting inside from the left wing, and although he found the net only seven times that season he effectively demonstrated the dashing style which was to make him one of Liverpool's most prolific goal-scorers.

As he grew in experience his influence on the team burgeoned. He was muscular and skilful, blessed with a sprinter's speed and a fearsome shot, good in the air and unfailingly courageous. He took the eye whether lining up on the left, the right or in the centre, a veritable one-man forward line. Sadly the side did not progress at the same rate and Billy – by now a Scotland regular whose international standing and durability were recognised by selection for Great Britain against the Rest of Europe in 1947 and 1955 – was in the unfortunate position of being a star in a team which plunged first to mid-table mediocrity and ultimately, in 1953/54, to relegation.

He reacted with characteristic determination and in his first four seasons in the lower grade notched 101 goals in 156 League matches – he was the Reds' leading scorer in eight out of nine seasons in the fifties – but it was not enough to secure promotion.

As his pace waned with age, he lost that stirring ability to run past defenders but compensated with a more mature passing game from a deep-lying position. The devotion of the supporters never wavered and when he returned at the age of 37 after one of several spells on the sidelines, he scored two spectacular goals against Bristol City in August 1959. The acclaim was rapturous, and deservedly so.

But there was more to Billy than his athletic attributes. A chivalrous, loyal man who was not too proud to stud the boots for his team-mates when left out of the side in 1959, he was always ready to help youngsters and went on to become a youth worker, lay preacher and JP. If ever a footballer deserved to be called a hero, then it was Billy Liddell. He will be forever revered on Merseyside and beyond.

BORN: Dunfermline, 10.1.22. GAMES: 537. GOALS: 229.
HONOURS: League Championship 46/7. 28 Scotland caps.

## 1945/46 — 1960/61

# JOHNNY WHEELER

The twin peaks of Johnny Wheeler's career were both behind him when he arrived at Anfield as one of the first signings of new Liverpool boss Phil Taylor in September 1956. Three years earlier the cultured right-half had played for Bolton Wanderers in the celebrated 'Matthews Final' at Wembley and in 1954 he had won his solitary England cap. But although Johnny's prime had gone, he still had plenty to offer an Anfield outfit locked in perennial struggle to escape from the Second Division, and on joining his home-town club he immediately gave value for money.

Johnny, an adaptable performer who spent much of his first term with Liverpool as an inside-right playing behind his fellow forwards, was a graceful prompter, precise of pass, firm of tackle and never short of attacking ideas. He was not a heavy scorer but sometimes surprised goalkeepers with snap shots, one of his most memorable being a 20-yard drive past Harry Gregg in an FA Cup defeat by Manchester United in 1960. Port Vale, though, have best reason to remember his striking powers. With nine minutes remaining of a Second Division encounter at Anfield in November 1956, the score was 1–1. Enter Johnny with a hat-trick in five minutes to transform the game.

On the debit side, there were times when quickness of thought was not matched by fleetness of foot. If possession was lost, Johnny's recovery was not always rapid, which resulted in pressure on the defence, but more often his experience made him a joy to play alongside. He spent only one season, 1958/59, as captain – before the job passed to his cousin, Ronnie Moran – but he continued to exert a major influence, using his vast experience to nurse youngsters through their early matches.

In autumn 1959, aged 31, he was sidelined by injury and then suffered a spell of indifferent form. The end appeared to be nigh but he fought back with some fine displays under new boss Bill Shankly, eventually giving way to youth in the form of Gordon Milne. Johnny, a kind and humorous character who went on to be trainer and assistant manager of Bury, won no medals at Anfield but can look back on a thoroughly professional and worthwhile stint.

BORN: Liverpool, 26.7.28. GAMES: 177. GOALS: 23.
HONOURS: 1 England cap.

OTHER CLUBS: Tranmere Rovers 48/9–50/1 (101, 9);
Bolton Wanderers 50/1–55/6 (189, 18).

## 1956/57 — 1961/62

# ALAN ARNELL

## 1953/54 — 1960/61

The scoring rate of Alan Arnell would be enough to have many modern managers reaching feverishly for their chequebooks. But the big, rangy centre-forward, who averaged a fraction short of a goal every two games for Liverpool during the middle and late fifties, never established himself as a regular in the side.

Alan – who was blooded by the Reds as an amateur, perhaps a sign of desperation in the quest for talent to lift the club back into the top flight – had all the attributes expected of a typical front-line bustler of his era. He was strong, energetic and good in the air; his touch on the ball, while not delicate, was respectable and his distribution was adequate. During his most prolific campaigns, 1955/56 and 1956/57, he scored 23 times in 37 League outings yet failed to convince successive managers, Don Welsh and Phil Taylor, that Billy Liddell would be better employed on the wing than leading the line.

Some contemporary observers reckon Alan was short of aggression and lacked the necessary drive to elbow aside even the challenge of fellow striker Louis Bimpson – who had a similarly unsatisfying Anfield career despite contributing plenty of goals – let alone those of the altogether more accomplished Dave Hickson and Roger Hunt at the end of the decade.

Nevertheless Alan Arnell had his triumphs, notably a brave hat-trick after pulling a muscle early in the game at Huddersfield in 1956, before going on to maintain his strike-rate in the lower divisions.

BORN: Chichester, 25.11.33. GAMES: 75. GOALS: 35.

OTHER CLUBS: Tranmere Rovers 60/1–62/3 (68, 33); Halifax Town 63/4 (14, 6).

## FRED MORRIS

Fred Morris was a tall, dashing right-winger whose neck-or-nothing style was beloved of supporters; he was a clean striker of the ball who scored some rousing goals; and he was a joker, his face usually split in a wide grin.

In short, Fred was a soccer character. Unfortunately, despite several stirring displays – a two-goal show against Leyton Orient at Anfield in November 1959 comes to mind – he didn't have enough class to make the grade with Liverpool.

Fred was signed from Mansfield Town by Phil Taylor in March 1958 for £7,000. He was then 28 and had perhaps spent too long in the lower reaches of the League to make a successful transition.

After missing the first two games of the following season he played 40 without a break, netting a dozen times in the process, a creditable achievement. He was injured early in 1959/60 and had just reclaimed his place when Bill Shankly moved in at Anfield. Fred played in the next match – a 4–0 drubbing by Cardiff City – and was never selected again.

BORN: Oswestry, 15.6.29. GAMES: 48. GOALS: 14.

OTHER CLUBS: Walsall 50/1–56/7 (210, 43); Mansfield Town 56/7–57/8 (57, 17); Crewe Alexandra 60/1 (8, 1); Gillingham 60/1 (10, 1); Chester 61/2 (29, 3).

## 1958/59 — 1959/60

## BOBBY CAMPBELL

The end of season 1959/60 came too soon for Bobby Campbell. The constructive wing-half was enjoying his most effective run in the Liverpool side and although the arrival of Tommy Leishman and Gordon Milne made his future challenging, to say the least, there were some grounds for optimism.

As the Reds completed their League programme with a 3–0 home victory over Sunderland, Bobby was in his element. His neat, creative skills were beginning to mesh impressively with fellow providers Jimmy Melia and Johnny Wheeler and his tackling, never his strongest feature, was taking on a promising crispness. Sadly, his impetus was shattered by the summer recess and never regained. He made only one more senior appearance for Liverpool before joining Portsmouth.

The major flaws in Bobby's game were a marked lack of pace and, because he was at his best going forward, a tendency to be lured out of position. This was never better illustrated than against Cardiff City in December 1959 when, offered the chance to create a favourable early impression on new boss Bill Shankly, he was given the runaround by Derek Tapscott. Bobby went on to become a coach and manager with some success.

BORN: Liverpool, 23.4.37. GAMES: 14. GOALS: 1.

OTHER CLUBS: Portsmouth 61/2–65/6 (61, 2); Aldershot: 66/7 (5, 0).
MANAGER: Fulham, Portsmouth, Chelsea.

## 1959/60 — 1960/61

# DICK WHITE

For four seasons, as Liverpool knocked in vain on the door of the First Division, Dick White was the calm and valiant kingpin of a generally resolute defence.

The first link in the Reds' illustrious Scunthorpe connection, which was to lead the likes of Ray Clemence and Kevin Keegan to Anfield, Dick was a part-timer at the Old Showground when he was signed by 'Pool boss Don Welsh in November 1955 as a prospective long-term replacement for stalwart stopper Laurie Hughes.

The veteran responded with spirit to the challenge of youth and Dick was allowed only sporadic opportunities during his initial 18 months on Merseyside. He made the most of his time though, helping his new club take the Central League title in his first full season, and when Laurie finally bowed to the inevitable, Dick appropriated the number five shirt with relish, missing only two League matches between 1957/58 and 1960/61. He built a reputation as a dependable, unspectacular centre-half who was willing to assume responsibility and able to carry it well. As befitted a six-footer, he excelled in aerial combat but, as with so many of his ilk, distribution was not his strong point.

Dick rarely suffered a chasing but when pressurised – Tom Johnston of the excellent, underrated Leyton Orient side and Graham Moore of Cardiff City were two opponents of the late fifties who had the ability to stretch him – he stuck to his task with admirable tenacity.

Attack was never his forte and he scored only one goal in more than 200 Liverpool appearances, though he is remembered for one surging sortie which took him past three Orient defenders to lay on an injury-time winner for Roger Hunt in the FA Cup at Anfield in January 1960.

Dick's tenure in central defence ended, as did a spell as captain, with the advent of Ron Yeats in 1961/62, but he was both adaptable and quick enough to switch to right-back to win a Second Division title medal – two own-goals at Middlesbrough in the Reds' first defeat of the campaign provided a minor hiccup – before seeing out his career with Doncaster.

BORN: Scunthorpe, 18.8.31. GAMES: 216. GOALS: 1.
HONOURS: Second Division Championship 61/2.

OTHER CLUBS: Scunthorpe United 50/1–55/6 (133, 11);
Doncaster Rovers 62/3–63/4 (82, 0).

# 1955/56 — 1961/62

# JOHN MOLYNEUX

John Molyneux might have been the prototype for the popular image of a fifties full-back. Tall and solidly constructed, he was far removed from the modern breed of overlapping defender, but when it came to doing his primary job – keeping out the opposition – there could be few complaints about his work during his seven years at Anfield.

Indeed, for six of those campaigns John was a first-team regular, performing with credit for three managers. Initially he served Don Welsh for nearly two seasons after arriving from Chester for £4,500, and then saw out the three-and-a-half year reign of Phil Taylor. But perhaps the greatest measure of his ability is that Bill Shankly was content for him to retain the right-back berth for 18 months as the decade closed.

John's primary attributes were his strength in the tackle and an instinct for danger which made goal-line clearances a much-appreciated speciality. His distribution was efficient and he formed a useful understanding with right-half Johnny Wheeler, but he could be exposed for lack of pace, a defect he normally managed to disguise by a cautious approach. Fleet-footed wingmen such as Peter McParland of Aston Villa and Middlesbrough's Edwin Holliday sometimes posed problems but on his day John could subdue the majority of Second Division speed merchants.

Getting forward was not one of his major concerns but he did allow himself the occasional flourish, one notable foray coming in an epic 4–4 draw at Villa Park in March 1960 when he scored one of his rare goals after combining, typically, with Wheeler.

John, a dedicated all-round sportsman, ultimately lost his place when Dick White moved to right-back in the Shankly reshuffle of 1961/62. He then returned to Chester for a second substantial spell.

BORN: Warrington, 3.2.31. GAMES: 249. GOALS: 3.
OTHER CLUBS: Chester 49/50–54/5 (178, 1) and 62/3–64/5 (67, 0).

## 1955/56 — 1961/62

# JIMMY HARROWER

Jimmy Harrower was blessed with a treasure trove of natural ability; sadly the Anfield career of the stocky Scottish inside-forward failed to do justice to his extravagant gifts.

When Phil Taylor persuaded Hibernian to part with the ball-playing under-23 international for £11,000 in January 1958, the Liverpool manager was optimistic that he had secured a man capable of scheming the Reds' return to the First Division. There were few apparent defects to Jimmy's game. His ball control was magnetic, his passing majestic; he possessed a savage, if sometimes wayward shot and he was strong with a low centre of gravity which made knocking him off the ball seem like removing a limpet from a rock.

The one superficial flaw was a lack of pace, for which it was reasonably reckoned his other talents would compensate. Several early displays confirmed his potential and one exhibition against Stoke in April 1958 had the Kop drooling as he stroked the ball around, giving full expression to his repertoire of delicate chips, lobs and dummies.

Unfortunately he could not attain consistency and often drifted through games making scant contribution, perhaps not benefiting from the presence of another play-maker, Jimmy Melia. The two repeatedly made pretty patterns together as they interchanged passes but this joint artistry frequently led nowhere in terms of team advantage.

An abrasive aspect to the Harrower game also surfaced. This sometimes provoked altercations, such as the petty series of skirmishes with Tom Casey of Bristol City which led to a booking in August 1959. More unwelcome was a certain cockiness which was entertaining when it took the form of saucy flicks and daring through-balls but unsavoury when it descended, on occasion, into petulance and the taunting of less skilful opponents.

As first Phil Taylor and then Bill Shankly explored every option in the push for promotion, Jimmy was tried on the wing and as a deep-lying centre-forward, a role in which he shone briefly. Eventually Shankly opted to look elsewhere for inspiration and sold his fellow Scot to Newcastle for £15,000. An unusually unfulfilling Anfield sojourn was at an end.

BORN: Alva, Clackmannanshire, 18.8.35. GAMES: 105. GOALS: 22.

OTHER CLUBS: Hibernian; Newcastle United 60/1–61/2 (5, 0); Falkirk; St Johnstone; Albion Rovers.

## 1957/58 — 1960/61

# DAVE HICKSON

There have been some sensational Merseyside transfer tales in recent decades – those involving Alan Ball, Kevin Keegan and Ian Rush spring to mind – but none created a greater furore than the sale of Everton idol Dave Hickson to Liverpool in November 1959. When Dave crossed Stanley Park, which separates the two grounds, feelings ran so high that some Everton fans swore they would follow him and defect to the old enemy, while a contingent from the Kop pledged to make the opposite journey in protest at the £10,500 deal.

Dave – Phil Taylor's last signing before handing over to Bill Shankly – was a fiery, buccaneering centre-forward, a man obsessed with scoring goals, whose distinctive blond thatch had stood out like a beacon in the Blues' attack during two successful spells. The stage was thus set for a bold entrance and Dave obliged with a show that was pure theatre. He bagged both goals – one a glorious diving header – in a 2–1 win over Division Two pace-setters Aston Villa and exuded such charisma that the Anfield crowd cheered his every touch. Having transformed Liverpool's lacklustre season into one seething with possibilities, he consolidated with a run of dashing displays which yielded 21 goals in 27 games.

Big Dave had been coached by the legendary Dixie Dean, as his aerial work bore witness, but he actually boasted a respectable all-round game. One of his most lasting contributions to the Reds' cause was his part in the development of Roger Hunt, whom he gladly relieved of some of the scoring responsibility, and Roger still recalls him as one of the most effective partners he ever had. Dave continued to score freely in his second Anfield campaign, before the arrival of Ian St John made him surplus to requirements and he took his talents to fresh fields.

During his travels he was dubbed soccer's stormy petrel, a reference to assorted clashes with referees, but his only major offence in a Liverpool shirt was a sending-off for retaliation – he was a constant victim of provocation – against Sheffield United, after which he was cleared of deliberate violent conduct. A quiet man off the pitch, Dave Hickson deserves to be remembered as a footballer, not a fighter.

BORN: Ellesmere Port, 30.10.29. GAMES: 67. GOALS: 38.

OTHER CLUBS: Everton 51/2–55/6 (139, 63) and 57/8–59/60 (86, 32); Aston Villa 55/6 (12, 1); Huddersfield Town 55/6–56/7 (54, 28); Cambridge City; Bury 61/2 (8, 0); Tranmere Rovers 62/3–63/4 (45, 21).

## 1959/60 — 1960/61

# ALAN A'COURT

In full flight, left-winger Alan A'Court was a stirring sight. When he hared for the byline and crossed the ball at full stretch, he was one of the most difficult customers to confront Second Division full-backs in the late fifties.

He wore a number nine shirt for his Liverpool debut at Middlesbrough in February 1953 but his speed, directness and capacity to provide accurate centres marked him out as a natural wingman. Accordingly, with Billy Liddell usually occupying Alan's favoured left flank, the youngster drifted in and out of the side during his first two seasons in serious contention for a place, getting a chance only when the Scottish international switched wings or was selected at centre-forward.

Alan established himself during the Reds' first season following relegation to the Second Division and was a linchpin in the struggle for promotion which was to last for eight campaigns. He remained a regular for half of Liverpool's initial term back among the elite in 1962/63 before giving way temporarily to Kevin Lewis. His first-team ambitions were finally extinguished when the richly promising Peter Thompson was signed in August 1963. Alan could be expected to scrap for a place with Kevin but, at such a late stage in his career, there could be no contest with the brilliant Peter.

Although never a prolific scorer, Alan packed a strong shot and had a knack of finding the net when it mattered. Liverpool were on the threshold of promotion in March 1962 when they found themselves two down with ten minutes to go in the vital confrontation with fellow high-fliers Leyton Orient at Brisbane Road. In stepped the faithful A'Court with a brace of point-saving goals, neither as spectacular as his memorable strike against Chelsea in the FA Cup earlier that year, but of crucial importance.

By then Alan was perhaps beginning to go past his peak and it was easy to forget there had been a time when his left-flank fire, control and consistency had looked likely to win him a place in the game's higher echelons. He played five times for England, including three appearances in the 1958 World Cup Finals in Sweden, before becoming one of several players who lost out to the emerging Bobby Charlton – Bolton's Doug Holden and Edwin Holliday of Middlesbrough suffered a similar fate.

But failure to become an international star should not detract from Alan's achievements at Anfield before he left to see out his playing days at Tranmere and coach at Norwich, Chester, Crewe, Stoke and in Zambia. The teenager who caused a stir in his rugby-loving family by choosing soccer as his livelihood gave distinguished and loyal service to Liverpool. His deeds on the field spoke for themselves but he was also an inestimable asset to the club behind the scenes, keeping morale bubbling with his infectious humour and encouraging young players such as Ian Callaghan. Football would be the richer for more men like Alan A'Court.

BORN: Rainhill, Lancashire, 30.9.34. GAMES: 382. GOALS: 63.
HONOURS: Second Division Championship 61/2. 5 England caps.

OTHER CLUBS: Tranmere Rovers 64/5–65/6 (50, 11).

## 1952/53 — 1964/65

# BERT SLATER

**1959/60 — 1961/62**

Bert Slater was fearless, agile and short. Unfortunately it was the last-mentioned characteristic which seemed to be constantly in the spotlight during his early days as Liverpool's number one goalkeeper.

The modest, 5ft 8½in Scot arrived at Anfield as part of the transaction which took his predecessor, Tommy Younger, to Falkirk in the summer of 1959, and made a chequered start with his new club. After performing heroics at Cardiff on his debut, Bert blundered once against Bristol City and then twice against Hull. He was replaced by Doug Rudham and returned to the side only when the South African was injured.

After several more alarming incidents, for which his lack of inches was usually blamed, Bert improved and eventually hit brilliant form. During the following term he was an ever-present and conceded only 27 goals in the first 29 games of the 1961/62 promotion campaign before surprisingly being axed – to the consternation of some team-mates – in favour of Jim Furnell. Throughout that fine run he displayed exceptional handling on the ground and missed little in the air, benefiting enormously from an instant understanding with the dominant new centre-half, Ron Yeats.

There was clearly no future for Bert at Anfield and he returned to Scotland to prove his class in Dundee's progress to the 1963 European Cup semi-finals. In 1965 he headed south again to join Watford and defied Liverpool in an epic FA Cup draw two years later. When he moved into coaching he could look back on an accomplished career.

BORN: Musselburgh, Midlothian, 5.5.36. GAMES: 111. GOALS: 0. HONOURS: Second Division Championship 61/2.

OTHER CLUBS: Falkirk; Dundee; Watford 65/6–68/9 (134, 0).

# TOMMY LEISHMAN

## 1959/60 — 1962/63

Long-striding, fierce-tackling Scot Tommy Leishman presented a menacing prospect when he arrived at Anfield in November 1959, just two weeks ahead of Bill Shankly. Gangly and gaunt, his dark features accentuated by a severe crew-cut, Tommy would have been a natural to play a trainee undertaker, if only he had been an actor! Instead he was destined for a relatively short, but effective tenure as Liverpool's left-half.

Tommy was signed from St Mirren, with whom he had won a Scottish Cup medal earlier that year, as a £9,000 replacement for Geoff Twentyman, whose role had not been satisfactorily filled since he had joined Ballymena United in the twilight of his career. A part-timer during his Saints days, Tommy thrived under Shankly's more rigorous training regime and quickly impressed with a promising display against Charlton at Anfield.

He was quick off the mark, good in the air and always eager for the ball, though his distribution lacked the imagination and precision that were the hallmarks of his eventual successor, Willie Stevenson. Nevertheless Tommy, a very left-sided performer, was a regular choice for two and a half seasons, including the 1961/62 promotion campaign in which his drive and enthusiasm were important assets.

He played 11 games on Liverpool's return to the top grade but lacked the class essential for a tilt at the Championship. When Shankly opted for Stevenson, Tommy returned north of the border to play well for Hibernian before becoming player-manager of Irish club Linfield.

BORN: Stenhousemuir, 3.9.37. GAMES: 119. GOALS: 7. HONOURS: Second Division Championship 61/2.

OTHER CLUBS: St Mirren; Hibernian; Linfield. MANAGER: Linfield.

# KEVIN LEWIS

**1960/61 – 1962/63**

The Anfield career of Kevin Lewis was a perplexing affair. Playing almost exclusively as a winger, he averaged better than a goal every two games and yet failed to find a niche as Bill Shankly built his great side of the mid-sixties.

The lanky flankman was recruited from Sheffield United in 1960 when Billy Liddell was on the verge of retirement and Ian Callaghan was adjudged too inexperienced. Kevin immediately began justifying his £13,000 fee, netting on his debut at home to Leeds and going on to notch 19 goals in 32 games. He thus became top scorer in his first term at Anfield – no mean feat with the likes of Hunt and Hickson in the side.

During the promotion campaign that followed, sharpshooter Kevin remained prolific. He scored in half his 20 games but was displaced by Callaghan and wasn't offered another run until midway through 1962/63 in Division One. Among the elite, he netted regularly and often spectacularly, only to be rewarded by Peter Thompson's arrival. Not surprisingly, he departed – to Huddersfield – perhaps wondering what was needed to cement a Liverpool place.

A versatile performer – he scored two when standing in at centre-forward for the suspended Ian St John when the Reds clinched promotion against Southampton – he was quick, skilful and good in the air but was at times easily brushed off the ball and inclined to be unpredictable.

Despite an outwardly casual manner, Kevin was nervous before games and may not have been temperamentally suited to the big time. He was lost to the British game when, still only 25, he emigrated to South Africa.

BORN: Ellesmere Port, 19.9.40. GAMES: 81. GOALS: 44. HONOURS: Second Division Championship 61/2.

OTHER CLUBS: Sheffield United 57/8–59/60 (62, 23); Huddersfield Town 63/4–64/5 (45, 13); Port Elizabeth, South Africa.

# JOHNNY MORRISSEY

# JIM FURNELL

Life was not easy for an aspiring young winger at Anfield as the fifties drew towards a close. If he somehow managed to sidestep the great Billy Liddell and long-established Alan A'Court, there were still the likes of Ian Callaghan, Kevin Lewis and Fred Morris to contend with.

Even so, the denizens of the Kop reckoned they saw something special when little Johnny Morrissey broke through to the fringe of the team. He showed hardness unusual in a wingman, allied his pluck with cunning, carried a ferocious shot and was blessed with all-round, natural talent. To confirm his place in their hearts, he hailed from the tough Scotland Road area of the city; in short, he was one of their own.

Limited chances during an unexpectedly brief Liverpool career allowed him to display his abilities to only intermittent effect but he was clearly a player of potential and it shocked supporters when he moved – to Everton, of all clubs – for £10,000 in August 1962.

There were rumours of strife over the deal between the board and Bill Shankly, who was said to be keen to keep Johnny. Feelings among the fans ran higher still as he helped the Blues win the League Championship in his first season at Goodison Park before going on to give ten years' distinguished service to Harry Catterick's team.

BORN: Liverpool, 18.4.40. GAMES: 37. GOALS: 6.

OTHER CLUBS: Everton 62/3–71/2 (259, 43); Oldham Athletic 72/3 (6, 1).

Liverpool rescued Jim Furnell from the nether regions of professional football – where he had performed creditably but hitherto anonymously for Burnley's reserve teams for more than half a decade – and plunged him straight into the hunt for promotion in February 1962.

The popular Bert Slater had been controversially dropped and Jim, who had been limited to two League outings with the Turf Moor club by the consistency of Adam Blacklaw, came in for the final 13 games of the campaign. He let no one down and the Reds duly made it to the First Division, where Bill Shankly initially kept faith with his £18,000 acquisition.

Though he rarely inspired the confidence of his defenders in the way his predecessor had, Jim held on to his place in the top flight until he broke his finger 13 games into the season, an injury which effectively signalled the end of his Anfield career. He was replaced by Tommy Lawrence, who proved to be an infinitely superior performer, and moved to Arsenal a year later. Jim enjoyed a creditable mid-sixties spell with the Gunners before going on to do well with Rotherham United and, particularly, Plymouth Argyle, for whom he played until he was 39.

BORN: Clitheroe, Lancashire, 23.11.37. GAMES: 28. GOALS: 0.
HONOURS: Second Division Championship 61/2.

OTHER CLUBS: Burnley 59/60–60/1 (2, 0); Arsenal 63/4–67/8 (141, 0); Rotherham United 68/9–69/70 (76, 0); Plymouth Argyle 70/1–75/6 (183, 0).

## 1957/58 — 1960/61

## 1961/62 — 1963/64

# JIMMY MELIA

Everything had gone Jimmy Melia's way in 1963, a year in which the creative inside-forward's subtle promptings had helped lift Liverpool into a Championship-challenging position by late December. He was the ideas man of a side well on the way to becoming one of Britain's best, and though just turned 26, had already played nearly 300 times for the Reds. His advance had recently been recognised with two England caps and, with such a blend of quality and experience, Jimmy seemed to be hovering on the very edge of greatness.

The soccer fates, however, are nothing if not unpredictable. A minor ankle injury sidelined the prematurely balding schemer shortly before Christmas and Bill Shankly was forced to make a radical change to his line-up. There was no obvious replacement for Jimmy so he improvised, moving Ian St John into a deep-lying position to take some of the midfield responsibility and introducing Alf Arrowsmith to partner Roger Hunt up front. Ian and Alf revelled in their new roles and though Jimmy made a brief and unconvincing reappearance when he regained fitness, his Anfield days were done.

But this rather abrupt exit should not obscure the earlier achievements of a player of enviable natural skills, who had celebrated his debut with a goal against Nottingham Forest in December 1955 and in the following seasons established himself in a side perpetually pushing for promotion. The 1958/59 term, in which he netted 21 times, was a personally productive one but his most impressive form was reserved for 1961/62, when the Reds finally left Division Two behind them.

At his best Jimmy Melia was one of the most constructive players Liverpool ever had, combining flair, industry and intelligence. He was the master of the penetrating through-pass and was adept at shielding the ball, though there were times when he retained possession too long and a delicate dribble might take him past the same opponent twice.

Such over-elaboration antagonised the Anfield fans, normally such an inspiration, and he was on the receiving end of some unreasonably barbed criticism. An occasional tendency to drift out of a match in which he had made a bright start also infuriated Kopites, who traditionally favoured players with a little more obvious fire about their games than Jimmy's more measured approach. The abuse was particularly scathing when Jimmy missed a penalty five minutes from time against Brighton at Anfield – with the visitors a goal up – in October 1959. As ever, he demonstrated commendable resilience in the face of adversity and had the satisfaction of nodding the equaliser seconds ahead of the final whistle.

The same fortitude saw him survive the disappointment of a short, unsuccessful stint with Wolves before giving admirable service to Southampton, whom he helped to reach the First Division in 1966. There was to follow a wandering managerial career, perhaps the sweetest moment of which was the unceremonious ejection of Liverpool from the FA Cup by his Brighton side on the way to Wembley in 1983.

BORN: Liverpool, 1.11.37. GAMES: 287. GOALS: 78.
HONOURS: League Championship 63/4. Second Division Championship 61/2.
2 England caps.

OTHER CLUBS: Wolverhampton Wanderers 63/4–64/5 (24, 4);
Southampton 64/5–68/9 (139, 11); Aldershot 68/9–71/2 (135, 14);
Crewe Alexandra 71/2 (4, 0). MANAGER: Aldershot; Crewe Alexandra;
Southport; Brighton and Hove Albion; Stockport County.

## 1955/56 — 1963/64

# RONNIE MORAN

Ronnie Moran's inspired backroom work as Liverpool evolved into the dominant power in English football has tended to overshadow his playing career, a circumstance which does grave injustice to one of the Reds' sturdiest bulwarks throughout a testing period of their history and on to the dawn of the glory days.

A burly full-back with a penchant for dead-ball situations – his left foot was a devastating weapon from the penalty spot and at free kicks – Ronnie ranks high among Anfield's most enthusiastic and effective defenders down the years. Indeed, some shrewd contemporary observers maintain that he should have won more representative honours than a brace of appearances for the Football League.

Ronnie's ample build might have suggested a lack of pace but he covered ground with deceptive speed and was rarely caught out. Strong in the tackle and combative in the air, he was a reassuring sight when his side came under pressure and his presence was never more appreciated than at Eastville in December 1959 when a rampant Bristol Rovers threatened to rout the Reds. The visiting defence wobbled visibly, with the notable exception of Ronnie, who made three goal-line clearances and numerous last-yard tackles, as Liverpool went on to win with two breakaway goals – a victory due largely to their left-back.

In his early days Ronnie concentrated so avidly on his defensive skills that he was rarely found in attack, but confidence came with maturity and he grew more adventurous. Ipswich bore the brunt of one telling excursion at Anfield in 1959 when he surged upfield, found Fred Morris on the wing and ran on to nod Fred's centre down for Roger Hunt to net.

Ronnie had made his League debut for an indifferent Liverpool outfit at Derby in November 1952, but failed to claim a regular place during the two-year struggle against relegation which ended unsuccessfully in the spring of 1954. His breakthrough came half-way through the first, acclimatising term in the lower grade when he ousted Frank Lock. He then missed only six League outings in the following five campaigns and enjoyed a spell as skipper at the end of the decade as his team strained unremittingly to escape from Division Two.

Sixteen months of injury problems then removed him from the action and, with promotion finally beckoning, he seemed likely to miss out on the triumph after striving for so long to achieve it. But he returned to fitness just in time to earn a richly-deserved medal in 1961/62.

There was even better to come. In the Reds' second season back in the top flight they lifted the title and Ronnie capped his career by playing in 35 games on the way to the trophy. By now, though, he really was slowing down and in 1964/65 Chris Lawler came in at right-back, with Gerry Byrne switching to Ronnie's left-flank slot.

But one last bonus awaited the old campaigner before he turned his attention to coaching the club's youngsters. Byrne broke his collar-bone in the FA Cup Final against Leeds and Ronnie was called up to do battle in two European Cup semi-final encounters with mighty Inter Milan, giving a good account of himself against the brilliant Brazilian, Jair. It was a fitting end to the playing days of one of the most dedicated one-club men who ever drew breath.

BORN: Liverpool, 28.2.34. GAMES: 379. GOALS: 16.
HONOURS: League Championship 63/4. Second Division Championship 61/2.

## 1952/53 – 1964/65

# GORDON MILNE

Gordon Milne was the first Shankly signing destined to play a role in Liverpool's triumphant march through the early and mid sixties. He arrived with none of the fanfares which greeted the subsequent entrances of Ian St John and Ron Yeats but in his own way he was as crucial a cog in the Anfield machine as his more famous team-mates.

A stocky and industrious right-half, Gordon was never a player to grab a game by the scruff of its neck and dominate it. He was the fetcher and carrier of the side, rather like a middle man in a relay race; the job he did was indispensable to the team effort but he was rarely the centre of attention when it was time to hand out the plaudits.

Gordon's approach was neat and unflashy, like the man himself. He was not a ferocious tackler, relying on anticipation to make interceptions before setting up attacks with admirably precise distribution. He was adept at brisk one-two manoeuvres, a style which complemented the often more ambitious, probing methods of Willie Stevenson on his left.

Some believed that for a man who popped up so often around the opposition's penalty box Gordon did not find the net regularly enough, but though his haul was admittedly on the meagre side, he had the knack of scoring vital goals. Match-winning efforts on the way to the 1965/66 title against fellow contenders Burnley, Leeds and Manchester United were typical.

Gordon was bought from Preston in August 1960 and Bill Shankly could be unusually certain that he was getting value for his £16,000. He had known the Lancashire lad from the cradle and watched him grow up – having been a Deepdale colleague of Gordon's father, Jimmy, during his playing days – and judged that he was acquiring a 'hardy little boy who would fight for the Liverpool cause'.

In fact, Milne Junior made an indifferent start with his new club. After being preferred to the experienced Johnny Wheeler for an early eight-game run, he was ousted by the veteran, who was enjoying something of an Indian summer. But Gordon fought back with spirit, as Shanks knew he would. By March 1962 he had regained his place and, growing in confidence all the time, was an ever-present in the Second Division title campaign that followed.

His performances had assumed a reassuring consistency and he won two Championship medals, but suffered the abiding disappointment of missing the 1965 FA Cup victory through an injury sustained in a 4–0 Good Friday defeat at Stamford Bridge. The only sad image of an otherwise glorious Wembley occasion was of a forlorn and soggy Milne, seated on the bench in his track-suit in the pouring rain as the team of which he was normally such an integral part enjoyed one of its finest hours.

In 1967 Gordon was allowed to move up the coast to Blackpool although many supporters felt that, while his form had dipped, he still had plenty to offer. But Shankly had decided that his side, which was betraying slight hints of a relative slide, needed surgery and that, at 30, the dapper wing-half was needed no more. Gordon, after a brief sojourn at Bloomfield Road, went on to an enterprising career in management.

BORN: Preston, 29.3.37. GAMES: 277 (2). GOALS: 19.
HONOURS: League Championship 63/4, 65/6.
Second Division Championship 61/2. 14 England caps.

OTHER CLUBS: Preston North End 56/7–60/1 (81, 3); Blackpool 67/8–69/70 (64, 4). MANAGER: Wigan Athletic; Coventry City; Leicester City; Besiktas, Turkey.

## 1960/61 — 1966/67

# GERRY BYRNE

When Bill Shankly breezed into Anfield in December 1959, the career of full-back Gerry Byrne was going nowhere rather too quickly for comfort. After making only two first-team appearances in two seasons and performing but moderately for the reserves, the swarthy defender was on the transfer list and looked for all the world like a player who would loiter on the fringe of the big time for several years before drifting inevitably towards a lower grade of football.

The new boss, however, saw something that everyone else had evidently missed. He transformed Gerry from a Central League plodder into one of the most effective backs in the land – and although he couldn't have known it at the time he was breathing life into the future of a man who, one rainy day in May 1965, was destined to become one of the true heroes of Liverpool soccer history.

But even the most inspired manager needs a little help from fate, and it came in the form of injuries to regular left-back Ronnie Moran. Gerry stepped in with a string of accomplished performances and, when Ronnie returned to first-team duty, continued his development by switching to right-back at the expense of Dick White.

He was an ever-present in the 1961/62 promotion campaign and became an automatic choice throughout the heady triumphs of the mid-sixties, reclaiming his left-sided role when Chris Lawler replaced the ageing Moran. Quiet and undemonstrative in both play and demeanour, Gerry brought a granite reliability to the Reds' defence. He wasn't over-endowed with pace but compensated by reading the game with cool assurance and with a tackle that was fearsome. Shankly was adamant that there wasn't a harder – or fairer – footballer in the game and, never a man prone to understatement, described his protégé's performance in the defeat of Belgian champions Anderlecht in late 1964 as 'the best full-back display Europe has ever seen'.

The match which clinched Gerry's place in Liverpool legend was the 1965 FA Cup Final against Leeds United in which he played for 117 minutes with a broken collar-bone, overcoming grinding pain and disguising his infirmity from Don Revie's men, who would certainly have taken advantage if they had recognised his plight. Not only did he subdue the lively Johnny Giles, he also laid on the Reds' first goal in extra time when he took a glorious pass from Willie Stevenson, reached the byline and swept over a cross for Roger Hunt to head home.

Having played a full part in taking two Championships as well as the Cup triumph, Gerry hurt a knee against Leicester City in August 1966 and was never quite the same dominant force again. When recurring knee trouble prompted premature retirement in 1969, leading to a spell as an Anfield coach, Shanks was again warm in his praise: 'When Gerry went, it took a big chunk out of Liverpool. Something special was missing.'

For a man who enjoyed so much success at club level, Gerry had little international joy. In the first of his two outings for England he endured a chasing from Scotland's Willie Henderson, and he perhaps lacked the class to mount a serious challenge to the immaculate Ray Wilson. Liverpool, though, knew his value – and it was immense.

BORN: Liverpool, 29.8.38. GAMES: 329 (1). GOALS: 3.
HONOURS: League Championship 63/4, 65/6.
Second Division Championship 61/2.
FA Cup 64/5. 2 England caps.

# 1957/58 — 1968/69

# ROGER HUNT

It was the night they dubbed him 'Sir Roger'. More than 60,000 people had sallied forth in torrential rain, forsaking the comforts of hearth and home to bid farewell to one of Liverpool's favourite sons. Never mind that he had left the club more than two years earlier; he would have a place in their hearts forever. It was the testimonial match for one of the all-time great goal-scorers, and no one wanted to miss the party.

Those locked out on that emotional evening in April 1972, when Anfield's capacity stood at 56,000, were left to listen to the roars from within and reflect on the supreme importance of Roger Hunt to the Reds throughout the fabulously successful sixties – a decade in which his goals had been their staff of life.

Roger's rise was little less than meteoric after scoring on his debut – as a 21-year-old with only amateur football and five Central League games behind him – against Scunthorpe at Anfield in September 1959. He quickly secured a regular place, netting 21 times in 36 games. In 1961/62 his prolific partnership with Ian St John was born and Roger struck 41 times in 41 outings, including five hat-tricks, to play a crucial role in turning the Reds' promotion dream into reality. Division One didn't know what was about to hit it.

The next six years brought an avalanche of goals – 149 in a mere 229 League games, to be precise – and it's no coincidence that Liverpool won the Championship in Roger's two most prosperous campaigns. In fact in 1965/66, the season of their second title triumph, the Reds didn't lose a First Division match in which he scored.

But there was more to Roger Hunt and his value to Liverpool than mere statistics. The explosive shot, the sudden and destructive pace, the strength which made him so hard to dispossess and his phenomenal work-rate were all well known. Less appreciated, perhaps, were his accomplished but unflashy ball control, neat distribution, refusal to hide from the ball when things were not going his way and an agile soccer brain which might have made him effective in a deep-lying role.

Goal-getting, though, was his golden gift and he employed it to the full. Never afraid to miss, Roger scored spectacular goals and easy goals, those that he bludgeoned into the net, like the brutal volley that jolted Inter Milan in the 1965 European Cup semi-final at Anfield, and those that he caressed past the 'keeper, such as the subtle touch that deceived Manchester United's Alex Stepney at Old Trafford in 1968.

His England record – 18 goals in 34 games, which included only two defeats – was outstanding, though he never received due credit for that, perhaps because he replaced national hero Jimmy Greaves in the 1966 World Cup. That Roger was the least-lauded member of Alf Ramsey's team was the outrageous product of ignorance and bias, and it was scandalous that such a selfless player should be driven to voluntarily end his England tenure as a result of constant and often hysterical criticism.

Modest to a fault and even-tempered, Roger was a referee's dream. The only moment of controversy came in March 1969, when he was substituted in an FA Cup defeat by Leicester and hurled his shirt into the dugout in frustration – a wholly untypical incident. By then he had survived a post-World Cup dip in form to bounce back for a brief but bountiful liaison with Tony Hateley before his Liverpool days tailed off as Bill Shankly sought new faces to end a relatively lean period. In December 1969 the 31-year-old Roger moved to Bolton, the club he had supported as a boy, to close a career which had seen him shatter the Reds' scoring record and bring unprecedented glory to the club. The fans loved him for it; a knighthood was the least they could offer . . .

BORN: Golborne, Lancashire, 20.7.38. GAMES: 484 (5). GOALS: 285.
HONOURS: League Championship 63/4, 65/6.
Second Division Championship 61/2. FA Cup 64/5. 34 England caps.

OTHER CLUBS: Bolton Wanderers 69/70–71/2 (76, 24).

# 1959/60 — 1969/70

# IAN ST JOHN

Ian St John was the spark that lit a flame destined to burn triumphantly for the next three decades and beyond. When quizzed by his board about the wisdom of paying Motherwell £37,500 for the Scottish international centre-forward, Bill Shankly described him as the man the Reds couldn't afford *not* to buy, the most urgently needed component of his brave new team. The manager's judgement, as usual, was impeccable.

From the night of Ian's first appearance in a red shirt – a Liverpool Senior Cup Final against Everton at Goodison Park in August 1961 – it was clear that he and his new club were made for each other. He moved with a jaunty swagger, 5ft 7½in of concentrated aggression topped by a pugnacious crew-cut – and he scored a hat-trick. His rapport with the fans was instant and complete; a folk hero was born.

The opening matches of the Division Two title campaign showed that Ian needed time to adjust but there was no doubting his quality. He was strong, cunning and courageous, devastating in the air for such a small man and adept at delicate flicks which did much to promote a fruitful scoring partnership with Roger Hunt. Ian notched 18 goals as the Reds went up, following that with 19 as a First Division new boy and 21 in 1963/64, on the way to the Championship.

That season saw a turning point which meant 'The Saint' would never score as heavily again but would contribute even more significantly to the eternal Anfield trophy quest. When schemer Jimmy Melia was injured, Shankly withdrew Ian into a deep-lying role in which he revealed his full potential for the first time. He became mastermind of the attack, feeding colleagues with possession and creating space for them to use it with his intelligent running. It didn't mean the goals dried up entirely – witness the jack-knife header which won the FA Cup against Leeds in 1965 – but simply that Ian's vision, mobility and all-round skills were employed to bring a new dimension to Liverpool's game.

Hunt continued to be prime beneficiary of his former front-running comrade's talents, as he acknowledged after scoring against Standard Liège in the European Cup Winners' Cup tie in December 1965. Ian had run half the length of the field, drawing defenders with him, before slipping the ball through for an unmarked Roger to net.

By the dawn of the seventies, with the Reds' first wave of Shankly-inspired honours behind them, Ian was into his thirties and his fitness had declined, but, used sparingly, he remained capable of transforming a game with his subtle touch and slick, close passing. Rumanians Dynamo Bucharest were the victims in December 1970 when he was taken off the bench to turn a shaky 1–0 lead into a comfortable 3–0 margin by laying on two late goals in the European Fairs Cup.

Throughout his playing days 'The Saint' was no stranger to controversy. He was often criticised for flashes of bad temper, such as the clash with Preston's Tony Singleton in March 1962 which led to a joint dismissal, but fire was an integral part of his make-up and, crucially, there was never malice aforethought.

On retirement he tried coaching and then management but didn't excel as many people thought he might and eventually became a TV personality. But in years to come it should not be as Jimmy Greaves' chat show sparring partner that he is recalled. In assessing his place in Liverpool's modern history, students of the Reds would do well to heed the wisdom of one Bill Shankly when he said: 'In the beginning was Ian St John . . .'

BORN: Motherwell, 7.6.38. GAMES: 418 (5). GOALS: 118.
HONOURS: League Championship 63/4, 65/6.
Second Division Championship 61/2. FA Cup 64/5. 21 Scotland caps.

OTHER CLUBS: Motherwell; Coventry City 71/2 (18, 3);
Tranmere Rovers 72/3 (9, 1). MANAGER: Motherwell; Portsmouth.

## 1961/62 – 1970/71

# WILLIE STEVENSON

Frustration with life in the shadow of Jim Baxter drove Willie Stevenson from his native Scotland to the other side of the world, but he was to find his true niche much closer to home. The lanky left-half – as slim as Jim and with a similarly cultured style – had won League and Cup medals with Glasgow Rangers before being ousted by the arrival at Ibrox of the gifted but mercurial Baxter. Unwilling to languish in the reserves, Willie adventurously elected to sample soccer in Australia and it was while he was on loan Down Under that Bill Shankly stepped in.

The Reds had made a lacklustre start to their first campaign after regaining Division One status and the manager recognised that more class and creativity were needed. Accordingly he secured Willie for £20,000 in October 1962, outbidding Preston North End in the process, and then displayed admirable patience as his countryman took time to adjust to the demands of the English game. Willie was obviously skilful but the pace of First Division life was too hectic for him and intolerant fans demanded the recall of Tommy Leishman. Shankly, as imperturbable as ever, kept faith with his new signing and was to reap rich rewards.

As Willie settled he began to exert a compelling influence. His biting tackle was the equal of Leishman's but the constructive side of his game was a class apart. A keenly intelligent tactician, he could change the emphasis of attack with a raking wing-to-wing pass or, more deadly still, drive a stiletto-thrust to the heart of the stoutest defence with the most crisp and piercing of through-balls.

He was seen at his best when winger Peter Thompson joined him on the left side of the Reds' 1963/64 Championship-winning team. Peter was an ideal partner, adept at making the oblique runs which made the most of Willie's subtle ability to judge the weight and angle of a pass, and together they formed a crowd-pleasing duo.

The full Stevenson repertoire never received a better showcase than the FA Cup Final against Leeds United in 1965 when most observers made him man of the match. He revelled in the sweeping width of Wembley, with its bowling-green surface made lusher than ever by heavy rain, and did more than anyone to put Don Revie's dour side to the sword. Willie it was who strolled imperiously past two opponents and freed Gerry Byrne on the left for the full-back to lay on the first goal for Roger Hunt.

As the decade progressed, the one-time Ranger – a dressing-room joker who did much to boost team morale – continued to turn in immaculate performances, missing only nine games in four seasons and playing a valuable part in a second title triumph in 1965/66. The campaign that followed was an anti-climax for Liverpool but Willie, as consistent as ever, did not seem in imminent danger of the axe. It materialised, however, in the shape of Emlyn Hughes and the 29-year-old schemer, finding himself out of the side with little prospect of a quick return, moved to Stoke City in December 1968.

Some fans were outraged, as they were over Gordon Milne's exit, at what they saw as premature dismissal of a loyal favourite, but Shankly was nothing if not decisive. Willie, who missed out on an international career due to abnormally hot competition from the likes of Dave Mackay and Jim Baxter, thus left the club with plenty still to offer and spent six more years in the League. He will be remembered at Anfield as an entertainer in the classic mould, a thoroughbred who contributed royally to some of the Reds' greatest triumphs.

BORN: Leith, 26.10.39. GAMES: 237 (1). GOALS: 17.
HONOURS: League Championship 63/4, 65/6. FA Cup 64/5.

OTHER CLUBS: Glasgow Rangers; Stoke City 67/8–72/3 (94, 5);
Tranmere Rovers 73/4 (20, 0).

# 1962/63 — 1967/68

# ALF ARROWSMITH

Alf Arrowsmith was the shooting star who burst across the Anfield heavens to wreath himself in glory for four dazzling months before his brightness was abruptly and prematurely dimmed. He rose sensationally to prominence in the second half of 1963/64 when the Reds' midfield general, Jimmy Melia, was injured. Ian St John moved back to assume the play-making role and the exuberant Alf came in to form a dual spearhead with Roger Hunt.

He signalled his intentions with a four-goal blitz on Derby in the FA Cup and for the duration of the season the young Mancunian could do little wrong, finishing with 15 League goals in 20 games and a Championship medal. Playing with refreshing innocence and verve, he ran at defences with unnerving pace and strength, and often attempted the seemingly impossible with spectacular success. Several goals were thrashed home with savage power from acute angles, and a 12-yard back-heel which beat Chelsea at Stamford Bridge would have delighted Denis Law himself. Easier opportunities were sometimes spurned but a glittering future seemed to be in store.

It all went wrong that August in the Charity Shield clash with West Ham when Alf damaged a knee so badly that he was out of contention for the first half of 1964/65. Although he stayed at Anfield for another four years, he was dogged by injuries and never regained his impetus. A popular, down-to-earth lad, he went on to spells with Bury and Rochdale.

BORN: Manchester, 11.12.42. GAMES: 50 (4). GOALS: 24. HONOURS: League Championship 63/4.

OTHER CLUBS: Bury 68/9–69/70 (48, 11); Rochdale 70/1–71/2 (47, 14).

## 1961/62 — 1967/68

# GORDON WALLACE

Pocket-sized Scottish inside-left Gordon Wallace hogged the limelight in television's first *Match of the Day* when he scored twice – including an 87th-minute winner – against Arsenal at Anfield in August 1964. But that is undoubtedly a distinction he would trade for a small fraction of the glory predicted for him when he broke through to the fringe of the first team in 1962/63. Perhaps it was a typical piece of Shankly psychology when the perceptive Liverpool boss described Gordon as the nearest thing to Tom Finney since the war, but Bill was sincere in his regard for the abilities of a player whose career was cursed by brittle bones.

Gordon, also at home on the wing, was quick and skilful with a mesmeric body-swerve and on his debut at West Brom he tantalised England full-back Don Howe. When he deputised for appendix victim Ian St John and scored twice in the 1964 Charity Shield encounter with West Ham, it was the start of a six-goals-in-eight-days burst – including his brace on TV and two more against Reykjavik in the Reds' first European game – which might have established him at the top level. But Gordon then suffered a barren spell in his only extended run before a cruel succession of injuries ended his Anfield ambitions and he joined Crewe.

BORN: Lanark, 13.6.44. GAMES: 20 (1). GOALS: 5.

OTHER CLUBS: Crewe Alexandra 67/8–71/2 (94, 20).

## 1962/63 — 1966/67

# PHIL FERNS

No one can take away from Phil Ferns the achievement of winning a League Championship medal with Liverpool in 1963/64. He earned the honour by the sweat of his brow, making 18 appearances as Bill Shankly's squad was hit by injuries, without remotely suggesting that he had the necessary class to forge a career in the First Division.

He stood in for Willie Stevenson at left-half, his most comfortable position, for a run of four games early in the campaign, returning later to deputise first for Ronnie Moran and then for Gerry Byrne at full-back. His most memorable game during this spell was at Old Trafford in November 1963 when he subdued Bobby Charlton as his side recorded a vital 1–0 victory.

Phil, who was already 24 when he made his League debut at home to Manchester City in August 1962, was a rugged defender whose enthusiasm outstripped his ability. He was rather lacking in pace and ball skill but his versatility stood the Reds in good stead over three seasons. The emergence of younger players ended his usefulness at Anfield and he moved on, first to Bournemouth, for whom his son was later to play, and then to Mansfield.

BORN: Liverpool, 14.11.37. GAMES: 28. GOALS: 1.
HONOURS: League Championship 63/4.

OTHER CLUBS: Bournemouth 65/6 (46, 0);
Mansfield Town 66/7–67/8 (56, 1).

## 1962/63 — 1964/65

# RON YEATS

'Take a walk around my centre-half, gentlemen.' The gleeful invitation came from master of banter Bill Shankly, introducing his mountainous new signing to assembled pressmen at Anfield in the summer of 1961. The colossus in question was, of course, Ron Yeats, who had just arrived from Dundee United to become a cornerstone of the Liverpool legend.

Shankly's admiration for the 6ft 2in Scot dated back to his days in charge of Huddersfield Town, but the Yorkshire club hadn't had the brass to prise Ron from Tannadice. Thus, after failing in a bid for Jack Charlton of Leeds, the Reds' boss willingly parted with the required £30,000 for a man he was confident would put the fear of God into the Sassenachs. Having already tempted Ian St John south of the border, he had the backbone of his first great side.

Ron – inevitably nicknamed 'Rowdy' after Clint Eastwood's TV cowboy of that era – was made skipper within five months of his arrival and exercised monumental influence as the team galloped to promotion in his first season. Division Two centre-forwards seemed to be swallowed up by his all-pervading presence and even Sunderland's free-scoring Brian Clough, rampant against most opponents, was rendered ineffective.

Elevation to the top flight served only to emphasise Ron's talents. His aerial ability was awesome, his tackling thunderous and his distribution sensibly simple. Some said he was slow on the turn but, as Shankly revelled in declaring, not many attackers got past him to find out.

He led the Reds to two Championships and through a succession of stirring European adventures but reserved some of his most rousing personal performances for the victorious 1965 FA Cup campaign. In fact, it all nearly went wrong at West Brom in the third round when a whistler in the crowd gulled Ron into picking up the ball in his own penalty area. Justice was done when Bobby Cram missed the resultant spot kick.

In the fifth round at Bolton the Liverpool captain gave one of his bravest displays after pulling a muscle ten minutes into the match and going on to subdue the potent airborne menace of Wyn 'The Leap' Davies. He garnered further glory by laying on Roger Hunt's winner in the quarter-final against Leicester, and then comfortably snuffed out the threat of Leeds' Alan Peacock at Wembley.

As the sixties wore on the Yeats game, though still essentially rugged, acquired a little more polish and it was a rare adversary who could unsettle him. One who did was playing for Ajax on that infamous Amsterdam night in December 1966 when the Reds were eclipsed 5–1, but Ron was neither the first nor the last defender to be given a chasing by Johann Cruyff.

By the end of the decade Ron had turned 32 and was beginning to suffer back trouble, but when he eventually yielded his place to Larry Lloyd he still had the motivation to contribute a valuable stint at left-back.

Equal in stature to his footballing record were his off-the-field merits as skipper. Although he was quietly spoken, his imposing personality made him an impressive mouthpiece for colleagues in dealings with management, and he was a commendable influence on younger players.

These admirable attributes remain in the club's service in his current position of chief scout, but it is as an inspiring leader who never flagged that Ron Yeats will go down in Liverpool folklore; while 'Rowdy' stood firm there was always hope. He was, in the words of his mentor Bill Shankly, a fantastic man.

BORN: Aberdeen, 15.11.37. GAMES: 450 (1). GOALS: 15.
HONOURS: League Championship 63/4, 65/6.
Division Two Championship 61/2. FA Cup 64/5. 2 Scotland caps.

OTHER CLUBS: Dundee United; Tranmere Rovers 71/2–73/4 (97, 5).
MANAGER: Tranmere Rovers; Barrow.

# 1961/62 — 1970/71

# TOMMY LAWRENCE

It's always a pity to waste a good nickname, especially one as colourful as 'The Flying Pig', coined affectionately and with no trace of an insult by the Kop to describe their solidly-built sixties goalkeeper Tommy Lawrence. But it was an alternative epithet, less vivid but more precise and with a little added subtlety, which most aptly summed up the vastly underrated Scottish international; shrewd observers dubbed him the sweeper-keeper, a description which neatly captured his style and the way he fitted into the Liverpool system.

Tommy operated behind a back four which usually played square and which pushed upfield whenever possible. When it was breached by a penetrating pass or an opponent's run from a deep position, it was imperative to have a last line of defence capable of reacting instantly to the danger. This job called for anticipation, bravery and talent – qualities which Tommy possessed in abundance. There wasn't another 'keeper of his era better acquainted with the bootlaces of First Division forwards; diving at feet was his speciality and even when the likes of Law and Greaves were through with only Tommy to beat, it was never a formality.

The Reds were served royally by an intuitive understanding between their custodian and the mammoth centre-half Ron Yeats, who generally dominated the penalty area with his aerial strength. It was rare to see the two countrymen going for the same ball and while Ron was dealing with crosses, his unflappable 'keeper would be ready to protect the net with reliable handling and amazing agility for a man of his bulk.

Although Tommy was very much an under-praised stalwart throughout Liverpool's sixties triumphs, Bill Shankly was well aware of his value. He knew there were matches which his team won, apparently convincingly, but in which the scorelines were wholly misleading – thanks largely to the exploits of the undemonstrative Lawrence. One such was a 4–1 home win against Blackpool in the victorious 1965/66 Championship campaign. Alan Ball was rampant and threatened to overturn the title aspirants as he repeatedly sliced opened their defence with incisive service to Graham Oates and Ray Charnley. But the 'keeper was inspired, frustrating the Tangerines with a courageous and skilful display which enabled his side at first to survive and then to take both points.

By then Tommy was an experienced performer, having been first called to senior duty for the newly-promoted Reds – after five years at Anfield – when Jim Furnell was injured in October 1962. He instantly impressed, cementing his place with impeccable form and earning an early cap for Scotland against Eire in June 1963.

The following season brought a Championship medal and Tommy climaxed an accomplished first full term by brilliantly saving a George Eastham penalty, the turning point in the 5–0 thrashing of Arsenal which clinched the title. He built on this early success, earning a much-deserved reputation for consistency, and it was a double mystery that his international recall should have been delayed for six years and then been limited to a mere two matches when it finally arrived.

He remained Liverpool's first-choice goalkeeper until February 1970 – missing only five League games in eight seasons – when, in company with Ian St John and Ron Yeats, he finally gave way to the challenge of youth, having kept his successor waiting for two and a half years. The ultimate tribute to Tommy Lawrence is the identity of that young man who was made to wait so patiently – a certain Ray Clemence.

BORN: Dailly, Ayrshire, 14.5.40. GAMES: 387. GOALS: 0.
HONOURS: League Championship 63/4, 65/6. FA Cup 64/5. 3 Scotland caps.
OTHER CLUBS: Tranmere Rovers 71/2–73/4 (80, 0).

# 1962/63 — 1970/71

# GEOFF STRONG

It is one of football's ironies that Geoff Strong wanted to leave Arsenal because Gunners boss Billy Wright switched the goal-scoring inside-forward to a wing-half role. Yet when he settled at Anfield he found himself, at one time or another, in virtually every outfield position and rarely had a shirt to call his own.

Geoff had averaged more than a goal every two games during his Highbury spell and it seemed likely that Bill Shankly would use him as a striker alongside Roger Hunt in place of the seriously injured Alf Arrowsmith. But the £40,000 newcomer took time to adjust to the Reds' rigorous training regime and by the time he was fully fit the side had a formidably stable look about it.

But neither player nor manager was dismayed. Shankly was adamant that he had bought the Geordie for his all-round talent, not for any specific task, and Geoff proceeded to become one of the most effective utility players the British game has known. Indeed, as well as proving the most versatile man at the club, he also showed that he was one of the most talented. His midfield performances were notable for their skill and vision; at the back he was cool and resourceful; in the front line he demonstrated an instinct for goals backed by a savage shot.

Geoff's first major assignment on joining Liverpool was born out of heartbreak for Gordon Milne when the right-half suffered an injury which put him out of the FA Cup Final against Leeds. In stepped the player who was to become Anfield's master-of-all-trades, to be handed the critical job of neutralising the threat of Don Revie's midfield general Bobby Collins. So well did he fare that Collins had but minor impact and Geoff had time to test Gary Sprake with several stinging drives on his way to a winner's medal.

During the Championship campaign that followed, the ex-Gunner firmly established himself as the Reds' chameleon. At various times he stood in for Thompson, Stevenson, Lawler, Milne and Hunt; the only man whose position he did not cover was goalkeeper Tommy Lawrence, though if the green jersey had become vacant Geoff could doubtless have distinguished himself in it.

His finest hours that term came with two winning goals on the way to the final of the European Cup Winners' Cup, which Liverpool lost to Borussia Dortmund at Hampden Park. The first was a 25-yard thunderbolt off the underside of the crossbar against Juventus in the preliminary round; the second, scored despite a crippling knee injury, was a semi-final header past Celtic's Ronnie Simpson. Such heroics didn't go unnoticed by the Kopites, who chanted Geoff's name until he hobbled off the bench to take his bow when the title was clinched against Chelsea.

Over the next four years, as the manager began to experiment with his side, Geoff was an integral part of the set-up. In his final two seasons on Merseyside his wanderings were largely halted, with an accomplished tenure at left-back. If he had a particular forte, however, it was perhaps as sweeper, a role denied him by the eminence of Tommy Smith. But it was for the diversity of his talents that he was most missed when, at the age of 33, he moved to Coventry City. Geoff Strong didn't leave one gap – he left ten.

BORN: Newcastle, 19.9.37. GAMES: 193 (5). GOALS: 32.
HONOURS: League Championship 65/6. FA Cup 64/5.

OTHER CLUBS: Arsenal 60/1–64/5 (125, 69); Coventry City 70/1–71/2 (33, 0).

# 1964/65 — 1969/70

ALAN BANKS

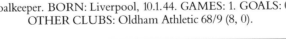

### ALAN BANKS 1958/59—1960/61

Centre-forward. BORN: Liverpool, 5.10.38. GAMES: 8. GOALS: 6.
OTHER CLUBS: Cambridge City; Exeter City 63/4–65/6 (85, 43)
and 67/8–72/3 (173, 58); Plymouth Argyle 66/7–67/8 (19, 5).

### ALAN JONES 1959/60—1962/63

Full-back. BORN: Flint, 6.1.40. GAMES: 5. GOALS: 0.
OTHER CLUBS: Brentford 63/4–69/70 (249, 2).

### BOBBY THOMSON 1962/63—1963/64

Full-back. BORN: Menstrie, Clackmannanshire, 21.11.39.
GAMES: 7. GOALS: 0. OTHER CLUBS: Partick Thistle;
Luton Town 65/6–66/7 (74, 0).

### PHIL CHISNALL 1964/65—1965/66

Forward. BORN: Manchester, 27.10.42. GAMES: 8. GOALS: 2.
OTHER CLUBS: Manchester United 61/2–63/4 (35, 8);
Southend United 67/8–70/1 (142, 28); Stockport County 71/2 (30, 2).

### BILLY MOLYNEUX 1964/65

Goalkeeper. BORN: Liverpool, 10.1.44. GAMES: 1. GOALS: 0.
OTHER CLUBS: Oldham Athletic 68/9 (8, 0).

ALAN JONES

BOBBY THOMSON

PHIL CHISNALL

BILLY MOLYNEUX

ALAN HIGNETT

TOM LOWRY

JOHN OGSTON

JOHN SEALEY

### ALAN HIGNETT 1964/65

Full-back. BORN: Liverpool, 1.11.46. GAMES: 1. GOALS: 0.
OTHER CLUBS: Chester 66/7 (6, 0).

### TOM LOWRY 1964/65

Full-back. BORN: Liverpool, 26.8.45. GAMES: 1. GOALS: 0.
OTHER CLUBS: Crewe Alexandra 66/7–77/8 (436, 2).

### JOHN OGSTON 1966/67

Goalkeeper. BORN: Aberdeen, 15.1.39. GAMES: 1. GOALS: 0.
OTHER CLUBS: Aberdeen; Doncaster Rovers 68/9–70/1 (70, 0).

### JOHN SEALEY 1964/65

Forward. BORN: Wallasey, 27.12.45. GAMES: 1. GOALS: 1.
OTHER CLUBS: Chester 66/7–67/8 (4, 0).

### DAVID WILSON 1966/67

Winger. BORN: Nelson, 24.12.42. GAMES: 0 (1).
GOALS: 0. OTHER CLUBS: Preston North End 60/1–66/7
(170, 31) and 68/9–73/4 (111, 10); Bradford City
*on loan* 71/2 (5, 0); Southport *on loan* 73/4 (2, 0).

DAVID WILSON

# PETER THOMPSON

When a sprightly, if rather distant Championship challenge withered in April 1963 – the Reds' first spring in the top flight for nine years – Bill Shankly made a momentous decision. He earmarked Peter Thompson as the one crucial ingredient missing from his title-winning recipe and signed the Preston winger, in the face of opposition from Juventus, Everton and Wolves, for a club record fee of £40,000. A year later Bill's mission was accomplished and the new man had played a thrilling part in the first of many triumphs before his Anfield days were done.

Peter Thompson was a soccer sorcerer, a pleaser of crowds and a teaser of full-backs. On his day he brought to the game a dancer's grace and the daring of a matador; when the Muse was not with him he was prone to over-elaboration and could be the most frustrating man afield. Unlike certain other gifted players, however, he offered no hint of the prima donna and he was never afraid of hard graft.

Despite being right-footed, Peter came into the side on the left flank where Alan A'Court and Kevin Lewis had both been judged deficient during the previous campaign. He made an eye-catching debut at Ewood Park, running at the Blackburn defenders, making them twist and turn in their efforts to stay with their elusive quarry and rendering an offside trap too perilous to contemplate. As autumn turned to winter and the points piled up, Peter and Ian Callaghan, whose more direct approach was in marked contrast to his own jinking and swaying, became the most formidable wing pairing in British club football.

The former Deepdale man's impact at Anfield could hardly have been greater, though there were those who said he should score more goals and that his final pass too often went astray. The fact was that his fierce shot *could* be a wayward weapon but his crosses, while not always matching the brilliance of his approach play, were as reliable as those of most contemporaries. There was also a theory that Peter should switch to the right to encourage him to reach the byline and cross with his favoured foot instead of being forced infield as he was on the left, but such a scheme took no account of the excellent Callaghan.

The nitpickers were predictably notable by their silence when Peter capped his first, richly rewarding term as a Red with his most devastating display to date. He scored twice and turned the Arsenal defence inside out as Liverpool made certain of the title, drubbing the Gunners 5–0 in front of an ecstatic Kop.

Peter's progress continued as Shankly's men lifted the FA Cup in 1965. His personal highlight was waltzing past Hollins and Hinton to grab the first goal in the semi-final against Chelsea with a fearsome left-foot drive between Bonetti and his near post. A second Championship medal soon followed but the nearest Peter came to further Cup success was in 1971, when he came on as substitute to breathe life into a hitherto dull final which Arsenal won to clinch the double. By then he was plagued by knee trouble and after a lot of time on the treatment table he moved to Bolton in November 1973. Surprisingly in view of past injuries, he was able to put in four spirited years before retiring.

One perennial gripe of Liverpool fans was Peter's banishment for long periods to the international wilderness. After starring in Brazil in 1964 his appearances were cruelly curtailed by Alf Ramsey's decision to do without wingers, though he did represent his country as late as 1970. But in the final analysis it is in a red shirt that Peter Thompson will be remembered – and as an entertainer, one of the finest of his time.

BORN: Carlisle, 27.11.42. GAMES: 404 (8). GOALS: 54.
HONOURS: League Championship 63/4, 65/6. FA Cup 64/5. 16 England caps.
OTHER CLUBS: Preston North End 60/1–62/3 (121, 20);
Bolton Wanderers 73/4–77/8 (117, 2).

## 1963/64 — 1971/72

# TONY HATELEY

When Tony Hateley opened his Liverpool scoring account with a rousing hat-trick against Newcastle on the second Saturday of 1967/68, Anfield was the place to be. The stadium was bulging with nearly 52,000 people, the air was heady with the scent of triumphs to come and the 'H Bombers' – Roger Hunt also scored two in the 6–0 victory – had signalled their arrival as partners to be feared with a show of ruthless efficiency.

Bill Shankly, alarmed by a barren campaign after three seasons of glory, had paid Chelsea £96,000 for Tony in the belief that the towering centre-forward would hit the target with sufficient regularity to arrest any slide before it gained momentum. But despite such a euphoric start – somewhat marred by a Hateley own-goal in a defeat at Highbury two days later – and the new signing's commendable strike-rate of a goal every two games, the expensive remedy was doomed to failure.

The problem was that Tony, a majestic header of the ball who needed constant aerial fodder to function, was utterly alien to Liverpool's style. That didn't bother Roger, who fed avidly off his knock-downs and enjoyed unaccustomed freedom as markers homed in on the big man, but the other players were used to a varied build-up along the ground. Understandably, after years of more subtle methods, they struggled to adjust to the tactic of repeatedly slinging high balls into the penalty area. Thus, when that approach was non-productive – as it often was against top-class defenders – the Reds were left with few options because Tony was too clumsy to employ a passing game. Lacking the control to hold the ball and the precision to lay it off, he was the rock on which many of Liverpool's attacks broke down.

Despite these shortcomings, Tony had his moments. Twice he netted three times in League matches, and went one better in an FA Cup replay against Walsall to finish the season with 24 goals. No one could accuse him of not doing *his* job, even if he failed to fit the team pattern, but it was no surprise when he was replaced – by Alun Evans – early in the following campaign and joined Coventry for £80,000. Through no fault of his own, an 'H Bomber' had backfired.

BORN: Derby, 13.6.41. GAMES: 56. GOALS: 28.

OTHER CLUBS: Notts County 58/9–62/3 (131, 77) and 70/1–71/2 (57, 32); Aston Villa 63/4–66/7 (127, 68); Chelsea 66/7 (27, 6); Coventry City 68/9 (17, 4); Birmingham City 69/70–70/1 (28, 6); Oldham Athletic 73/4 (5, 1).

## 1967/68 – 1968/69

# BOBBY GRAHAM

When Bobby Graham struck a hat-trick as a 19-year-old debutant against Aston Villa at Anfield in September 1964, the skilful Scot seemed to have the perfect platform on which to build a successful Liverpool career. In retrospect his explosive start more closely resembled a curse. Though Bill Shankly was far too wise to be carried away on the strength of one performance, the expectations of the fans were elevated to the heavens and the inexperienced Bobby was not equal to them. Although he scored in the next match, he then suffered a dozen blank games and, often bedevilled by injuries, dropped out of serious contention for the next four seasons as other strikers held sway.

But Bobby's chance came again – and this time he was ready. At the start of 1969/70 – with Hunt and St John nearing the end of their illustrious Anfield days, Hateley long gone and Evans injured – a more mature Graham was pitched into a side very much in a state of flux. Now he looked a different player to the boyish performer of half a decade earlier, adding new-found determination and confidence to his old virtues of pace and control.

That term Bobby was an ever-present, scoring 13 goals in a moderate campaign by Reds' standards, and there were even whispers of an international call. But ten games into the following season the Graham bandwagon, now moving so smoothly, came to an abrupt halt when he broke his ankle against Chelsea at Anfield. He didn't start another match for five months, by which time John Toshack was on the scene. When Kevin Keegan appeared in 1971/72 Bobby was effectively crowded out and, bowing to the inevitable, he joined Coventry City for £70,000.

A short spell at Highfield Road and an even briefer loan period with Tranmere preceded a move to his native Motherwell, for whom he excelled for four years and earned rich praise. Even then he was not finished, spending another four seasons at Hamilton until retirement at the age of 36. At Liverpool Bobby was an unfortunate footballer, struck down at his peak. How well he deserved his belated recognition north of the border.

BORN: Motherwell, 22.11.44. GAMES: 123 (8). GOALS: 42.

OTHER CLUBS: Coventry City 71/2–72/3 (19, 3);
Tranmere Rovers *on loan* 72/3 (10, 3); Motherwell; Hamilton Academical.

## 1964/65 — 1971/72

# ALUN EVANS

If ever a young player seemed set for greatness it was perky, flaxen-haired Alun Evans in the autumn of 1968. Bill Shankly had just made him the first £100,000 teenager in British soccer and he had started his stint as Liverpool centre-forward with two richly promising displays crowned by three goals. But four years later, Anfield dream in tatters and potential unfulfilled, the golden boy had gone.

It might all have been so different. Alun started as a 17-year-old prodigy with Wolves and impressed mightily during his brief Molineux interlude. He gave one particularly precocious performance against Liverpool, having the temerity to rattle Ron Yeats and score a goal in the process. The Reds' boss was not a man to ignore such talent and when Alun became available Bill made sure that Anfield was his destination.

He was bought as a long-term replacement for Tony Hateley and provided a stark contrast to his rather one-dimensional predecessor, bravery being the one quality they shared. Alun was quick and skilful, full of cute tricks and sudden changes of direction that threw defenders into disarray. The mop-topped newcomer quickly unveiled his effervescent armoury, scoring after ten minutes of his debut at home to Leicester and then netting two at Molineux in a 6–0 thrashing of his former employers.

Perhaps predictably, the young man's learning curve became more gradual and he managed only four more goals that season. The following campaign was one of total frustration, with injuries and a night-club incident – in which his face was badly scarred – sidelining him for long periods, but he returned to something like top form in 1970/71. Despite a cartilage operation, the result of playing on a bone-hard pitch in Bucharest, Alun scored ten League goals in 21 games and lit up Anfield with a brilliant hat-trick against Bayern Munich in the European Fairs Cup.

Fitness again eluded him in 1971/72, a term which brought but one highlight, a breathtaking half-volleyed goal in a Cup Winners' Cup defeat by Bayern. By then, though, he was in the shadow of Messrs Keegan and Toshack and took the road back to the Midlands, where a new start with Aston Villa was to add little joy to an unlucky, unsatisfying career.

BORN: Bewdley, Worcestershire, 30.4.49. GAMES: 104 (6). GOALS: 33.

OTHER CLUBS: Wolverhampton Wanderers 67/8–68/9 (21, 4); Aston Villa 72/3–73/4 (62, 11); Walsall 75/6–77/8 (87, 7); Hellas FC, Melbourne.

# 1968/69 — 1971/72

# IAN ROSS

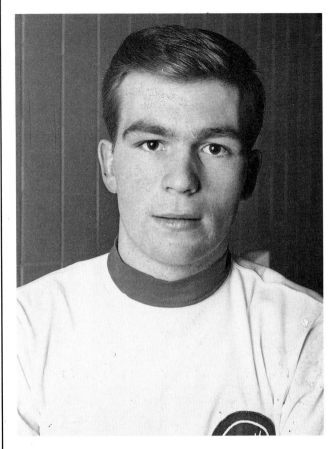

Any player who could subdue Franz Beckenbauer and Alan Ball and yet – unlike so many man-to-man markers – use the ball constructively when given the chance, would be guaranteed a first-team place at most clubs. Sadly for Ian Ross, it was not the case at Liverpool.

Ian, who eventually assumed the role of utility man vacated by Geoff Strong, made his debut as a substitute in January 1967. In the next two campaigns he stood in briefly for Smith, Byrne and Yeats at the back, impressing with reliability and skill, before Bill Shankly began to employ his tenacious qualities to shackle specific opponents. Ian did an effective job on Ball, then at his peak, when the Reds won 3–0 at Goodison in December 1969, but his finest achievement was the eclipse of 'Kaiser Franz' in a European Fairs Cup encounter with Bayern Munich in March 1971. He even found time to score Liverpool's only goal of the game as they reached the semi-final.

Ian enjoyed his longest unbroken run in 1971/72, wearing five different numbers during his spell of 20 games, before joining Aston Villa, for whom he performed with distinction alongside big centre-half Chris Nicholl. His success away from the hot competition of Anfield was well deserved.

BORN: Glasgow, 26.11.47. GAMES: 59 (9). GOALS: 4.

OTHER CLUBS: Aston Villa 71/2–75/6 (175, 3); Notts County *on loan* 76/7 (4, 1); Northampton Town *on loan* 76/7 (2, 0); Peterborough United 76/7–78/9 (112, 1); Wolverhampton Wanderers 79/80–81/2 (0, 0); Hereford United 82/3 (15, 0).

## 1966/67 — 1971/72

# DOUG LIVERMORE

Doug Livermore was a neat, workmanlike midfielder who simply didn't come up to the standard demanded at Anfield. He was handed the prompting role vacated by Ian St John when the Scot was axed after the Reds' shock FA Cup quarter-final exit at Watford in February 1970, and enjoyed a 13-match run to the end of the season as Bill Shankly set about reshaping his ageing team. His displays revealed strength, honesty and some skill but he lacked the pace and, most crucially, the inspiration for such an onerous task.

After that sequence Doug, who had made his debut as a substitute for Tony Hateley at Upton Park in April 1968, was never to start another League game for Liverpool and joined Norwich in November 1970 for £22,000. Carrow Road saw the best years of his playing career as he helped the Canaries gain promotion to Division One in his first full campaign in East Anglia.

Doug, who later saw service with Bournemouth, Cardiff and Chester, went on to become a respected coach and worked with the Welsh national team. He is currently assistant manager of Tottenham Hotspur, for whom he had a spell as caretaker boss between the reigns of David Pleat and Terry Venables.

BORN: Liverpool, 27.12.47. GAMES: 14 (3). GOALS: 0.

OTHER CLUBS: Norwich City 70/1–74/5 (114, 4); Bournemouth *on loan* 74/5 (10, 0); Cardiff City 75/6–77/8 (88, 5); Chester 77/8–78/9 (71, 6). CARETAKER MANAGER: Tottenham Hotspur.

## 1967/68 — 1970/71

# PETER WALL

# ROY EVANS

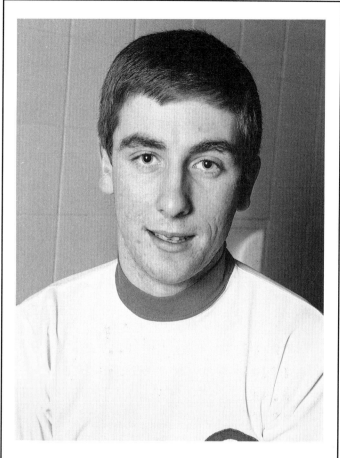

Peter Wall was a cultured defender who once seemed likely to succeed Gerry Byrne as Liverpool's long-term left-back. He arrived from Wrexham in October 1966 as the junior partner in a £26,000 full-back package which included Stuart Mason. But while Stuart was destined never to make a first-team appearance before returning to the Racecourse Ground, Peter made promising progress.

He made his debut at home to Burnley in March 1968, soon after Gerry had suffered the injury which was to end his career prematurely. Then, after makeshift stints by Tommy Smith and Ian Ross, Peter settled in for the remaining eight games of that season and the first 13 of the next. He revealed poise, skill and a calm assurance under pressure which perhaps veered too close to being casual for Bill Shankly's peace of mind, and Geoff Strong was handed the number three shirt for the duration of the campaign.

Peter, who perhaps needed a shade more drive for a top-rank career, resurfaced for a nine-match spell half-way through 1969/70 but didn't become established and joined Crystal Palace for £35,000. At Selhurst Park he found his niche and served the Eagles well for eight years.

BORN: Westbury, Wiltshire, 13.9.44. GAMES: 42. GOALS: 0.

OTHER CLUBS: Shrewsbury Town 63/4–64/5 (18, 0); Wrexham 65/6–66/7 (22, 1); Crystal Palace 70/1–77/8 (177, 3); Orient *on loan* 72/3 (10, 0).

The football career of Roy Evans stands as an inspiring example to any young professional with not quite enough ability to make it as a player at the top level. Roy was a skilful left-back who made his League debut against Sheffield Wednesday at Anfield in March 1970 as Geoff Strong's tenure was coming to an end and before Alec Lindsay became established. He was comfortable on the ball, passed well with his left foot and possessed boundless enthusiasm but lacked the necessary pace to make the position his own.

Roy hung on as a reliable stand-by for four frustrating seasons but looked destined for soccer oblivion until manager Bob Paisley stepped in with the offer of a job coaching the reserves. Still only 25, Roy must have been tempted to turn it down in favour of seeking a playing career elsewhere but perhaps felt, deep down, that Bob was being realistic.

Accordingly, he accepted the opportunity and worked hard to make the most of it, leading his charges to the Central League championship at his first three attempts and going on to repeat his success regularly in the eighties. Roy now works with the first team and has even been mentioned as a possible Liverpool manager of the future.

BORN: Bootle, 4.10.48. GAMES: 11. GOALS: 0.

## 1967/68 — 1969/70

## 1969/70 — 1973/74

# CHRIS LAWLER

Chris Lawler was hardly an eye-catching performer, seeming to saunter through games with all the apparent urgency of a man out walking his dog. There was no swagger, no tricks, no histrionics, but in time opponents came to realise – often ruefully, as they retrieved the ball from their net – that they ignored Liverpool's faithful right-back at their peril.

Not that his defensive capabilities weren't respected from the outset. It was obvious from early appearances deputising for centre-half Ron Yeats that the callow but composed Chris had all the qualities of a future back-four stalwart. No, what crept only gradually into the consciousness of opposing teams was an almost uncanny ability to ghost in behind his forwards and snatch goals when no threat seemed imminent. Presumably it was the result of instinctive anticipation, though sometimes it seemed like second sight.

The odd thing was that, unlike many defenders who pride themselves on finding the net, Chris was not a dead-ball specialist, never took penalties and did not possess a particularly powerful shot. Yet he can point to a career record of 61 goals, including ten in 1969/70 when he was the Reds' second-highest scorer, and 11 in European competitions, which saw some of his most famous efforts. His most prolific continental campaign was the 1965/66 Cup Winners' Cup in which he scored in three successive ties, starting with a deft header against Juventus before striking twice against Standard Liège and once against Honved.

Back in the First Division, Everton were twice the victims of the Lawler goal habit, both times at Anfield. In November 1970 Chris capped a stirring Liverpool comeback from a 2–0 deficit with a late winner, and the following season scored with an overhead kick to complete a 4–0 rout.

Priceless though these attacking diversions were, Chris never allowed them to distract him from his primary responsibilities at the back. In fact, he fulfilled them so well that he missed only one League game between October 1965 and November 1973 – and that was when he was rested before the 1971 FA Cup Final. He first came to prominence in the 1963 semi-final, slotting into the middle of a reshuffled defence alongside Yeats, and then earned widespread praise when he stood in for the skipper in three Easter victories during the title run-in a year later.

In 1964/65, when the ageing Ronnie Moran stepped down and Gerry Byrne switched to the left flank, Chris was handed the regular right-back berth. The slim, upright youngster took his chance with aplomb, underlining his progress by stifling the talents of speedy Leeds winger Albert Johanneson at Wembley and claiming a Cup-winner's medal. Calm, skilful and good in the air, Chris became a fixture and assisted in two Championship triumphs before a knee injury sustained at Loftus Road ended his proud record of consistency, effectively sidelining him for the rest of 1973/74. Despite a handful of appearances the following term he was never the same again and – after a move to Manchester City was called off by Liverpool at the last minute – he joined Portsmouth, later returning to Anfield for a coaching stint.

Chris's England outings were limited to four; there might have been more had he possessed a little extra pace. Some would point to competition from Keith Newton and Paul Madeley but Kopites would have none of it. For them, the man they called 'The Silent Knight' – a reference to his quiet, modest nature – was simply the best right-back in the business.

BORN: Liverpool, 20.10.43. GAMES: 546. GOALS: 61. HONOURS: UEFA Cup 72/3. League Championship 65/6, 72/3. FA Cup 64/5. 4 England caps.

OTHER CLUBS: Portsmouth 75/6–76/7 (36, 1); Stockport County 77/8 (36, 3).

## 1962/63 — 1975/76

# LARRY LLOYD

When strapping centre-half Larry Lloyd limped out of the Anfield action in early 1974, few observers could have guessed that the England international had played his last game for Liverpool. The thigh injury which had ended his interest in the encounter with Norwich City didn't seem serious and he was confidently expected to make a quick return.

It was never to be. The smaller but more skilful Phil Thompson was slotted in alongside Emlyn Hughes, bringing a continental style to the Reds' central defence, and the partnership prospered so fruitfully that Big Larry, an ever-present in the League Championship and UEFA Cup triumphs of the previous campaign, found himself discarded for good.

Bill Shankly bought the towering West Countryman, a dominant stopper in the Ron Yeats mould, from Bristol Rovers for £50,000 in April 1969. He saw him as the eventual successor to his vaunted colossus and so it proved. Larry made his entrance for a two-match spell when Ron was injured early in 1969/70, but it was not until the last six games of the campaign, when Shankly was breaking up his beloved sixties side, that the new man took his place on merit – and kept it until that fateful thigh strain changed the course of his career.

Larry confidently assumed the burden of replacing a Liverpool legend and, as his experience grew, showed there was more to his game than the obvious asset of aerial power. Though lacking pace, he was capable of using the ball well, especially with his left foot, and was exceptionally active in urging on his colleagues. His huge physical presence in opposition penalty boxes brought Larry disappointingly few goals but he did make one vital strike, heading what was to prove the winner against Borussia Moenchengladbach in the 1972/73 UEFA Cup Final.

Despite being out of the side already, Larry was devastated at missing the 1974 FA Cup Final and accepted a £225,000 move to Coventry three months later. He didn't settle there and Brian Clough got a bargain when he signed him for £60,000 in 1976. With Nottingham Forest Larry played a leading role in League Championship and European Cup glories and, for one match, won back his England place. A rare resurrection was complete.

BORN: Bristol, 6.10.48. GAMES: 217. GOALS: 5.
HONOURS: UEFA Cup 72/3. League Championship 72/3. 4 England caps.

OTHER CLUBS: Bristol Rovers 68/9 (43, 1); Coventry City 74/5–76/7 (50, 5);
Nottingham Forest 76/7–80/1 (148, 6); Wigan Athletic 80/1–82/3 (52, 2).
MANAGER: Wigan Athletic; Notts County.

# 1969/70 — 1973/74

# EMLYN HUGHES

A new adjective should be invented for Emlyn Hughes; nothing in the dictionary adequately captures the essence of a man possessed by an almost demonic fervour for football in general and Liverpool in particular. Enthusiastic, energetic, ebullient – they've all been used and deserve to be discarded. Ask his old Anfield team-mates and they'll tell you that mere words could never do justice to the man who led them to some of their most memorable triumphs.

Emlyn's arrival in February 1967 marked the beginning of the end of an era. Bill Shankly was making his first, tentative moves to dismantle his great sixties side and the bubbly Barrow boy, who made a handful of appearances at left-back in place of the injured Gerry Byrne before permanently replacing left-half Willie Stevenson for 1967/68, was the first newcomer to claim a regular place.

Shanks' admiration of the rookie Hughes began one spring day in 1966 when he watched the 18-year-old – who was to become, in the lurid language of the Reds' boss, 'one of the major signings of all time' – make his debut for Blackpool. Bill was so impressed that he made a £25,000 offer straight after the game but had to wait ten months before securing his quarry for £65,000.

Having moved to Merseyside, Emlyn wasted no time in making an impact. In his first game, at home to Stoke City, he dominated Potters' play-maker George Eastham and four matches later he earned a famous nickname. From the day he felled Newcastle forward Albert Bennett with a rugby tackle – nothing malicious, more an example of youthful impetuosity – Hughes was branded 'Crazy Horse', a label that was his for keeps.

Not that such eccentric acts were needed to draw attention to a richly promising player, for whom Leeds were soon willing to offer Peter Lorimer in part-exchange. Built like a dreadnought and with strength to match, long-striding Emlyn rampaged around the football grounds of England like a frisky rhino. If subtlety was lacking in his early approach, and if he did occasionally commit himself to rash tackles, his vast potential was always evident. Left-sided but good with both feet, strong in the air and boisterously inspirational, Emlyn became known for his dynamic surges into enemy territory. Southampton were on the receiving end at Anfield in April 1971 when he broke up an attack in front of his own goal, played the ball wide and steamed up the centre of the pitch. Arriving with uncheckable impetus on the edge of the Saints' box, he cracked a first-time shot into the net. Irresistible!

In 1973/74 Emlyn replaced Tommy Smith as captain and moved into the centre of defence, forming an enterprising partnership with Phil Thompson. By this time his play had matured, his approach calmer and more reliant on anticipation than the buccaneering tactics of old. Though perhaps not as popular a skipper as Smith or Yeats, Emlyn was a motivator supreme, leading by example and unflagging in his zest. In five seasons in charge he held aloft two European Cups, one UEFA Cup, two League Championship trophies and one FA Cup. At such moments his all-embracing grin – so familiar since his emergence as a TV person – was an emblem of Anfield ascendancy although, always one to wear his heart on his sleeve, he could also radiate utter dejection more thoroughly than most. None who saw him drag himself up Wembley's 39 steps to accept an FA Cup loser's medal in 1977 will forget his despair.

Emlyn – who won more caps as a Red than anyone else – was an emotional performer and a magnificent one. When he moved to Molineux it was no surprise that he helped Wolves to League Cup glory. Somehow, though, that grin looked out of place above an old-gold shirt . . .

BORN: Barrow, 28.8.47. GAMES: 657. GOALS: 48. HONOURS: European Cup 76/7, 77/8. UEFA Cup 72/3, 75/6. League Championship 72/3, 75/6, 76/7, 78/9. FA Cup 73/4. 62 England caps.

OTHER CLUBS: Blackpool 65/6–66/7 (28, 0); Wolverhampton Wanderers 79/80–80/1 (58, 2); Rotherham United 81/2–82/3 (56, 6); Hull City 82/3 (9, 0); Mansfield Town 83/4 (0, 0); Swansea City 83/4 (7, 0). MANAGER: Rotherham United.

## 1966/67 – 1978/79

# RAY CLEMENCE

Ray Clemence was possibly the most important factor in Liverpool's continued success throughout the seventies. That assessment came from Bill Shankly, the man who paid Scunthorpe United £18,000 for the 19-year-old goalkeeper in June 1967 and then saw him rise to become one of the best – maybe, at his peak, the very best – in the world.

When Ray arrived at Anfield, Bill hinted that a first-team spot was there for the taking. But the canny Reds boss was either under-valuing the ability of 'keeper-in-residence Tommy Lawrence, which was not likely, or indulging in kidology to spur the new boy to greater efforts, which was. In the event Ray had to wait two and a half seasons to claim a place. By then, having tuned his talents to an irresistible pitch of readiness at the elbow of his helpful predecessor, he was itching to prove himself.

His early games were played behind giant, aerially-dominant centre-halves – first Ron Yeats, then Larry Lloyd – and Ray initially impressed with safe handling, sharp reflexes and a knack of getting down quickly to low shots. But as his confidence grew in subsequent seasons it was clear that he was a truly outstanding all-rounder; apart from a weakness in goal-kicking – which he worked on until it came up to scratch – there were no perceptible flaws. Ray combined a keen positional sense with shrewd anticipation, instinctively knowing when to leave his line and when to stay on it. This made for an unflashy technique but Shankly knew that acrobatics were a poor substitute for clean sheets and blessed the day he'd rescued Ray from Third Division obscurity.

Another immense Clemence virtue, so vital to the 'keeper of a team such as Liverpool which spent long periods in their opponents' halves, was concentration, and Ray possessed it in abundance. He regularly passed lengthy chunks of a match marooned behind one of the world's most niggardly defences without getting a touch of the ball, and it's a measure of his greatness that he could respond so magnificently when the need arose. Indeed, but for the positive approach of this compulsive shouter and organiser – which demanded involvement and sometimes made him more sweeper than 'keeper – he might have spent his Anfield years as the loneliest man in English football.

Statistical proof of Ray's excellence is plentiful. In his first full term, which ended with a brilliant display in the FA Cup Final defeat by Arsenal, he conceded only 22 goals in his 41 games to help his defence equal the First Division record of 24 in a season. The achievement was destined to be eclipsed, however, as Ray let in a miserly 16 in 1978/79. But it's saves rather than cold figures which live on in the memories of Reds fans, with penalty stops being particularly vivid. One in a goalless away leg against Dynamo Dresden on the way to winning the 1975/76 UEFA Cup, when he dived full-length to reach a firm, low shot, was a real heart-stopper.

Clem, a dedicated trainer who relished scoring in five-a-sides and dubbed himself 'The White Pelé', ended his 'Pool days on a surprising note in August 1981. Still at the peak of his powers, he announced the need for a new challenge and joined Spurs, for whom he made more than 250 appearances. It's hard to see, though, what he hoped to find in the way of motivation at White Hart Lane that was missing at Anfield.

Running parallel to his club exploits was an illustrious international career throughout which he vied for the England jersey with Peter Shilton. The debate about who was the better will rage forever; suffice it to say that Kopites, like Ray's new fans at White Hart Lane, were a touch peeved with England manager Bobby Robson's final verdict.

BORN: Skegness, 5.8.48. GAMES: 656. GOALS: 0. HONOURS: European Cup 76/7, 77/8, 80/1. UEFA Cup 72/3, 75/6. League Championship 72/3, 75/6, 76/7, 78/9, 79/80. FA Cup 73/4. League Cup 80/1. 61 England caps.

OTHER CLUBS: Scunthorpe United 65/6–66/7 (48, 0); Tottenham Hotspur 81/2–87/8 (240, 0).

# 1968/69 — 1980/81

# STEVE HEIGHWAY

When Steve Heighway burst irreverently on to a decidedly staid First Division scene in October 1970, it was like a fresh breeze sweeping through a musty bootroom. With Alf Ramsey still in and wingers largely out – the likes of George Best and Eddie Gray were gilt-edged exceptions – the cobwebs were gathering thick and fast. The established order needed a kick up the backside and Steve, an innocent abroad in the tough, serious world of professional football, delivered it in his own gloriously unorthodox style.

He arrived from non-League Skelmersdale to bring pace and width to the Liverpool attack – Steve was a winger despite wearing the number nine shirt – and it was soon clear that Bill Shankly had not burdened him with contemporary Division One protocol. Instead of laying the ball off and running for a return pass in the accepted fashion, Steve had the audacity to take players on, and it confounded them. Knees high and elbows pumping, he ran at defenders and went past them – again and again. Sometimes the Reds' raw flyer seemed to overstep himself and an opponent would be odds-on to rob him; but Steve, basin haircut bobbing and moustache bristling, would often find an extra spurt of speed, stick out a toe and skip away with the ball. His raking stride made it hard for defenders to recover and his ability to cross accurately at full tilt gave a thrilling new dimension to the Liverpool front line.

Shankly had resisted the challenge of other top clubs to sign the athletic amateur, but it was when Steve was safely installed at Anfield that the manager pulled his master stroke. It would have been easy to dismiss the young Irishman's dashing approach as fine for the Cheshire County League but altogether too naive for the big time. Shanks, though, was too wise for that; having spotted something special he was *not* going to allow it to be coached into oblivion.

Steve, who won his first Eire cap the night after making his Liverpool debut, quickly turned heads with two-footed talent which enabled him to cut inside opponents or nip past them on the outside. No one who saw him rescue an apparently lost cause in the Merseyside derby at Anfield in November 1970 had the slightest doubt about his pedigree. Everton were two up and coasting when Steve broke free to score from an acute angle; then he slipped past two defenders to make John Toshack's equaliser with a cross from the left wing. The Reds went on to win with a goal from Chris Lawler but it was Heighway who had turned the tide. He capped his first, exhilarating campaign – in which he had only rarely frustrated by over-elaboration – with a near-post shot which deceived Arsenal 'keeper Bob Wilson and gave Liverpool a short-lived lead in the FA Cup Final.

In the early years of his career 'Big Bamber' – a university graduate, as was Brian 'Little Bamber' Hall – at times seemed jaded but Shankly, that motivator supreme, was always able to supply the remedy, and the arrival of another star, the precocious Kevin Keegan, removed much of the pressure. By the mid seventies Steve, while less spectacular than in the past, had become an enviably consistent performer and spent much of his time in deep positions prompting the Keegan–Toshack tandem. His touchline breaks, however, continued to be a potent attacking option and one such sortie set up the first goal for McDermott in the 1977 European Cup Final.

At the end of the decade Steve, in his thirties and faced with stiff competition for a place, crossed the Atlantic to end his playing days before returning to Anfield to coach youngsters. If he brings half as much flair to his new task as he once displayed on the world's football fields, then Liverpool can look forward to an exciting future.

BORN: Dublin, 25.11.47. GAMES: 444 (23). GOALS: 76.
HONOURS: European Cup 76/7, 77/8, UEFA Cup 72/3, 75/6.
League Championship 72/3, 75/6, 76/7, 78/9. FA Cup 73/4.
34 Republic of Ireland caps.

OTHER CLUBS: Minnesota Kicks.

# 1970/71 — 1980/81

# BRIAN HALL

Brian Hall was the man who made an art form out of being unobtrusive – but let none doubt the value to Liverpool of this perpetually busy and consistent footballer throughout the first half of the seventies.

The diminutive Glaswegian claimed a regular place when Ian Callaghan suffered cartilage trouble in autumn 1970. Brian, whose previous League experience had been limited to substitute appearances, slotted neatly into the team on the right side of midfield, energetically foraging for the ball and passing it on with a minimum of fuss.

Bill Shankly was so pleased with the way the skilful, slightly round-shouldered deputy fitted into the team pattern that when Ian was fit again he returned in a central position, allowing Brian to continue in the wide role. The newcomer kept his place for the rest of the season, making light of a slight deficiency in pace, and saw the Reds through to Wembley when he adroitly hooked home an Alun Evans cross to beat Everton in the FA Cup semi-final at Old Trafford. Arsenal won the final but the future beckoned promisingly.

The following term proved to be one of consolidation for Brian, despite several spells out of the side, as Shanks' task of replacing his first great team neared completion. Honours came in 1972/73 with triumph in the UEFA Cup and a Championship medal, though Brian was ousted for much of that campaign and the one that followed by the newly arrived Peter Cormack. He fought back to play in the victorious FA Cup Final against Newcastle in 1974 and then enjoyed his most active season in 1974/75, missing only seven League games.

After that his first-team aspirations withered with the advent of Jimmy Case and Brian – a graduate who rejoiced in the nickname of 'Little Bamber', standing four inches shorter than 'Big Bamber' Heighway – departed for Plymouth and Burnley before becoming a teacher. He will go down as an untiring worker who didn't have that vital turn of speed which might have lifted him to a higher plane. But in the final analysis there'll be no complaints from Anfield about the days in a red shirt of the loyal, dependable and, yes, talented Brian Hall.

BORN: Glasgow, 22.1.46. GAMES: 196 (24). GOALS: 21.
HONOURS: UEFA Cup 72/3. League Championship 72/3. FA Cup 73/4.

OTHER CLUBS: Plymouth Argyle 76/7–77/8 (51, 16);
Burnley 77/8–79/80 (43, 3).

## 1968/69 — 1975/76

# ALEC LINDSAY

Alec Lindsay was a man with a golden gift. Sadly, apart from three glorious seasons when he was arguably the best left-back in the land, he failed to make the most of it.

The talent in question was for passing, accurately and over long distances, with his left foot. To the casual observer that might not seem such a spectacular blessing, but to anyone who has watched generations of defenders hopefully hoofing high balls in the general direction of their forwards it was an asset to be cherished.

Alec cost Liverpool £67,000 when he arrived from his home-town club of Bury in March 1969 and, like so many newcomers to Anfield from the lower divisions, went straight into the Central League 'finishing school'. He had been a wing-half with the Shakers and some respected judges were so impressed with his ball skills that they saw him developing along the lines of fellow Gigg Lane graduate Colin Bell.

After taking longer than many to settle with the Reds – Alec was not a 'natural' trainer – he made his debut and several more unremarkable appearances in midfield before switching to the left-back berth he was destined to grace so stylishly. He created a good impression with two spells in 1970/71, making the position his own in the following campaign when he forged one of the most profitable Anfield partnerships of the seventies. Much is heard of the Keegan–Toshack link but equally valuable, in a less obvious way, was Kevin's understanding with the resourceful blond defender. Alec's long, raking passes to his front-men, often bent teasingly around helpless opponents, were made for Kevin, who was adept at bringing them under instant control before creating his own brand of mayhem. The full-back seemed to sense where his nippy target was going to run, playing the ball into space intelligently and with perfect weight, and the tactic had a major influence in the Reds' UEFA Cup and League Championship double in 1972/73.

Come the 1974 FA Cup Final against Newcastle and Alec was still in tremendous form. He was under-employed at the back, courtesy of the Magpies' feeble attacking efforts, but was prominent on the overlap as the Reds surged forward. It was from one such foray that he made the crispest strike of his life, driving a ferocious cross-shot past 'keeper Iam McFaul, only to have his joy cut short by an offside whistle.

Such a minor disappointment did nothing to sour an accomplished season and when Joe Mercer, England's caretaker manager, drafted him into the national side that summer, the career of Alec Lindsay was at its zenith with, it seemed, only cloudless horizons ahead. True, he had never been the quickest player and perhaps lacked the stamina for the midfield role which might have made more of his creative leanings, but he tackled well, read the game shrewdly and had found a productive niche.

Unfortunately, disillusionment was not far away. Alec's form faded badly in 1975 and he was replaced, first by Phil Neal and then by Joey Jones. For two years he strove in vain to regain his spot before taking that trusty left foot, briefly, to Stoke and then on to the United States. The unhappy epitaph on the playing days of Alec Lindsay must be that many men of inferior ability managed to achieve much more.

BORN: Bury, 27.2.48. GAMES: 244 (2). GOALS: 18.
HONOURS: UEFA Cup 72/3. League Championship 72/3. FA Cup 73/4.
4 England caps.
OTHER CLUBS: Bury 64/5–68/9 (126, 14); Stoke City 77/8 (20, 3);
Oakland, USA.

## 1969/70 — 1976/77

# JOHN TOSHACK

John Toshack was the thinking man's version of that oft-maligned breed, the big, brave striker. While many of that ilk are strictly one-dimensional, ready to batter defences into submission or perish in the attempt, John ultimately offered – after much hard work – a more varied range of attacking possibilities. Of course, he had a distinct advantage over fellow members of the centre-forwards' union in that he was blessed for most of his Liverpool career with the presence of Kevin Keegan. The diverse talents of the towering Welshman and his nippy, opportunist partner combined to give the Reds many of their finest hours.

John, aged 21 and already an established international, was signed for £110,000 from Cardiff in November 1970 and quickly endeared himself to the Kop in the surest possible way – by dumping Everton on the seat of their pants. In one of the most rousing Merseyside derbies of modern times, John helped to erase a two-goal deficit, climbing high above the Blues' Brian Labone to head the equaliser before nodding down Alec Lindsay's cross for Chris Lawler to clinch an emotional victory.

Such exploits were clearly a recipe for deification by the fans, but John's immediate progress did not match his dynamic start. His last 18 games of the season, including the FA Cup Final defeat by Arsenal, failed to produce a goal and it was apparent that, though he was always a power in the air, other aspects of his game were in need of serious attention. To his credit John applied himself well and – boosted by Kevin's breakthrough – gradually acquired more all-round skills, of which accurate distribution was the most notable. He used his newly widened scope intelligently and often to devastating effect, laying on a steady stream of chances with subtle flicks to his effervescent accomplice and creating space by astute running off the ball.

But while this improvement enabled John to play an important role in winning six major trophies, his road to glory was rarely smooth. For most of his Anfield tenure he was dogged by a nagging thigh injury – only once did he exceed 30 League games in a campaign – and was engaged in perennial battle to defend his place. At various times he faced challenges from Graham, Evans, Whitham, Boersma, Waddle, Kennedy, Fairclough and Johnson, seeing off all but the latter two. In fact, his shirt returned to him so often that he eventually called it Lassie!

Despite sometimes dropping John, both Bill Shankly and Bob Paisley – who once agreed to sell him to Leicester only for the £160,000 deal to founder on a failed medical – liked him on duty for European encounters, in which he gave some of his finest performances. One of the most unexpected came in the 1972/73 UEFA Cup Final first leg at home to Borussia Moenchengladbach, for which Tosh had been omitted. The match was abandoned because of heavy rain but Shanks had spotted that the Germans were vulnerable in the air. Accordingly the six-foot target man was recalled for the rescheduled game and laid on two goals for Kevin.

John's most prolific term, though, was 1975/76 when he found the net 23 times, including three hat-tricks, on the way to a League title and UEFA Cup double. Thereafter fitness problems and hotter-than-ever competition for places preceded a move, as player-boss, to Swansea where phenomenal success put him on a management trail which was to take him all the way to Real Madrid. His stature as one of the greatest names in Welsh soccer history was confirmed.

BORN: Cardiff, 22.3.49. GAMES: 236 (9). GOALS: 95.
HONOURS: UEFA Cup 72/3, 75/6. League Championship 72/3, 75/6, 76/7.
FA Cup 73/4. 40 Wales caps.

OTHER CLUBS: Cardiff City 65/6–70/1 (162, 75);
Swansea City 77/8–83/4 (63, 24). MANAGER: Swansea City; Sporting Lisbon;
Real Sociedad; Real Madrid.

# 1970/71 — 1977/78

# PHIL BOERSMA

Throughout his seven seasons on the fringe of the Liverpool team, Phil Boersma always seemed to be fighting a losing battle. A speedy utility forward with plenty of skill, he occasionally came agonisingly close to bridging the gap between Central League and First Division but perpetually failed to convince first Bill Shankly and then Bob Paisley that he was any more than a handy man to have about the squad.

Phil first came into the reckoning on his 20th birthday in September 1969 when he was brought on as a substitute for Alun Evans during a League Cup defeat at Manchester City. Several League outings followed, but at a time of team transition and strong opposition for forward places, the curly-haired youngster failed to establish himself. He then made patchy progress over the next two campaigns, but in 1972/73 seemed on the verge of a breakthrough, playing 31 times and scoring 13 goals in all competitions to claim League Championship and UEFA Cup medals.

He might have spoilt his encouraging work and precipitated a premature end to his Liverpool days when he walked out on Shanks on FA Cup Final day in 1974. Phil was outraged that after he had been substitute in previous rounds, Chris Lawler was given the job at Wembley. The manager understood his player's disappointment and the differences were patched up, but the Merseysider continued to find himself on the edge of the action. Despite several settled runs, including one of 18 League matches in 1974/75, Phil remained Anfield's 'nearly man' and, pushed yet lower in the pecking order by the emergence of David Fairclough, finally relinquished his hopes of a long-term future with the Reds in December 1975 when he joined Middlesbrough for £72,000.

Liverpool had lost a player of some verve, as anyone who saw his spirited dash into the box to make a late winner for Kevin Keegan against Southampton at Anfield in March 1973 would confirm. But Phil's form was fitful and he wasn't helped by carping from over-critical fans. It may be that he was a split-second slower in reacting to opportunities than some of his international colleagues, but in truth he fared no better in the lower divisions and after injury forced early retirement he turned to coaching.

BORN: Liverpool, 24.9.49. GAMES: 98 (21). GOALS: 29.
HONOURS: League Championship 72/3. UEFA Cup 72/3.

OTHER CLUBS: Wrexham *on loan* 69/70 (5, 0);
Middlesbrough 75/6–76/7 (47, 3); Luton Town 77/8–78/9 (36, 8);
Swansea City 78/9 (18, 1).

## 1969/70 — 1975/76

# JACK WHITHAM

Too much time on the treatment table robbed Jack Whitham of his chance to build a career at Anfield – and deprived Liverpool of a possible long-term successor to Roger Hunt. Jack was a strong, all-action centre-forward who was signed from Sheffield Wednesday for £57,000 in April 1970, four months after Roger's departure. At Hillsborough he had averaged only a little under a goal every two games but, alas, there was a catch. Jack had never started more than 18 games in a season thanks to a soul-destroying injury record; whenever he struck a patch of good form he was invariably sidelined before he could realise his potential.

He made his Reds debut as a stand-in for Bobby Graham in a goalless draw against Newcastle United at St James' Park early in 1970/71 but was offered only limited opportunities for the rest of that campaign. His first settled run came half-way through the following season and he responded with five goals in eight games, including a powerfully-struck hat-trick in a 3–2 Anfield defeat of Derby.

This sequence ended – inevitably – with fitness problems. After a two-game absence he returned to score the only goal in a victory at Huddersfield in February 1972 before he was struck down again. Although Jack, who was particularly prone to muscle strains, was to remain at Anfield for another two years before joining Cardiff City, he was never to play another first-team game for Liverpool. His bad luck continued wherever he went and he eventually gave up football to run a pub.

BORN: Burnley, 8.12.46. GAMES: 16. GOALS: 7.

OTHER CLUBS: Sheffield Wednesday 66/7–69/70 (63, 27); Cardiff City 73/4–74/5 (14, 3); Reading 75/6 (19, 3).

## 1970/71 — 1971/72

# JOHN McLAUGHLIN

# ALAN WADDLE

There was a time when Bill Shankly thought the slim, almost frail figure of schemer John McLaughlin would loom large in the seventies as one of the foundations of his second successful side. Sadly Shanks' optimism proved groundless as John's career withered and died in the harsh, hectic reality of First Division life.

His chance came during a period of transition for the Reds at the turn of the decade. The old order, so masterly in the sixties, was now being swept away and places were there for the taking. John was drafted in for the last match of 1969/70, a defeat at Stamford Bridge, and was then given 33 games in the following League campaign to establish himself.

He took the role of midfield creator and occasionally looked the part, coolly employing his deft touch on the ball and ability to judge the weight of a pass to good advantage. But pace and stamina were lacking, too often leaving John apparently out of his depth and struggling to have any effect on proceedings. Having failed to make the most of his lengthy settled run, he faded away as new players came into contention for his place. Eventually, after a brief spell on loan at Portsmouth, a serious knee injury put him out of the game.

BORN: Liverpool, 25.2.52. GAMES: 53 (2). GOALS: 3.

OTHER CLUBS: Portsmouth *on loan* 75/6 (5, 0).

The Liverpool career of gangling centre-forward Alan Waddle was a brief, unremarkable interlude enlivened by one moment of pure, unadulterated glory. It came after 68 goalless minutes of a Merseyside derby largely dominated by Everton at Goodison Park in December 1973. Ian Callaghan broke free on the flank and put in a speculative cross which Alan toe-poked at full stretch past stranded 'keeper David Lawson to win the match. It was the 6ft 3in striker's only goal in 22 appearances for the Reds – all made either deputising for John Toshack or as substitute – before he set off on a decade of travels which took him to six other League clubs.

Alan, a cousin of England winger Chris Waddle, never showed the necessary class to merit a prolonged stay at Anfield but he at least bowed out of the big time in an important match. He was called to the colours when Steve Heighway was injured in the 1977 European Cup semi-final second leg against FC Zurich at Anfield, but had little chance to impress and five months later was on his way to Leicester City for £45,000. His most productive spell came as a Toshack recruit at Swansea, whom he helped to rise from the Third Division to the First.

BORN: Wallsend, 9.6.54. GAMES: 16 (6). GOALS: 1.

OTHER CLUBS: Halifax Town 71/2–72/3 (39, 4); Leicester City 77/8 (11, 1); Swansea City 78/9–80/1 (90, 34); Newport County 80/1–81/2 (27, 8); Mansfield Town 82/3 (14, 4); Hartlepool United 83/4 (12, 2); Peterborough United 83/4–84/5 (36, 12); Hartlepool United 84/5 (4, 0); Swansea City 84/5–85/6 (40, 10).

# 1969/70 – 1974/75

# 1973/74 – 1976/77

## IAN CALLAGHAN

If ever one player embodied the multitude of qualities which built Liverpool into one of the world's greatest clubs then, undeniably, Ian Callaghan was that man. From the day he made his debut as a teenager against Bristol Rovers at Anfield in April 1960 – receiving an ovation from team-mates, opponents, the crowd, even the referee – until his departure for Swansea nearly two decades later, he was, without ever being a star in the accepted sense, a shining example of everything a top footballer should be.

Ian's career divides neatly into two halves. He spent the sixties as an orthodox right-winger, one of the best in the country, before converting into a chugging dynamo in central midfield, a role which was to win him a belated international recall at the age of 35.

He made his bow as a diminutive professional of six weeks' standing with only four Central League games behind him. A man-size shirt hung loosely on his wiry frame but there was no suggestion of a little boy lost when he started to play. In that first match he revealed confidence, bags of natural ability and a precious instinct which told him when to hold the ball and when to release it. A golden future awaited but Bill Shankly was wary of prematurely pitching his gifted rookie into the maelstrom of League football. A season and a half passed before he was awarded a regular berth and then he helped to win long-coveted promotion.

Ian's game blossomed in the First Division. He formed a potent partnership with left-flank trickster Peter Thompson and the honours flowed. While Peter was more devious, Ian was fast and direct, making it his business to reach the byline and feed Roger Hunt and Ian St John with a diet of crosses which did much to nourish the Reds' goal tally.

Never a heavy scorer himself, Ian did contribute several memorable strikes. Particularly satisfying was an acute-angled sidefoot from a well-rehearsed free-kick routine involving Hunt and Willie Stevenson that stunned Inter Milan in the 1965 European Cup semi-final at Anfield, though more spectacular was a 30-yarder which sunk Everton in autumn 1963 as Shankly's men headed for their first Championship.

The watershed in the Callaghan career came in 1970/71. Liverpool were experiencing an indifferent patch but their reliable right-winger was playing as well as ever until a cartilage operation sidelined him for four months. In his absence, newcomer Brian Hall prospered and there were fears that Ian's days in a red shirt were numbered. Such qualms were not shared by the manager, who doubted neither his man's resilience, nor his capacity to adapt, and simply handed him a new job in midfield.

Ian responded by missing only four games in the subsequent five seasons, during which he was awarded the MBE, was voted Footballer of the Year and played a major part in placing untold strain on the Anfield trophy cabinet. His intelligence and enthusiasm, precise passing and limitless stamina were never seen to better effect and that return to the England side – he had been axed when Alf Ramsey abandoned wingers in 1966 – was a fitting reward. The cascade of tributes which followed genuinely puzzled the modest Cally, who felt his game had remained at the same consistent level throughout his years with the Reds.

When it was time to move on he could look back on an exemplary record. He had been the one common denominator in three fine teams, played more games than anyone in the club's history, never been cautioned by a referee and set a towering example of loyalty, dedication and skill. Ian Callaghan created a formidable standard; if others can meet it they will be great men indeed.

BORN: Liverpool, 10.4.42. GAMES: 843 (5). GOALS: 69. HONOURS: European Cup 76/7. UEFA Cup 72/3, 75/6. League Championship 63/4, 65/6, 72/3, 75/6, 76/7. Second Division Championship 61/2. FA Cup 64/5, 73/4. 4 England caps.

OTHER CLUBS: Swansea City 78/9–79/80 (76, 1); Cork Hibernian; Soudifjord of Norway; Crewe Alexandra 81/2 (15, 0).

## 1959/60 — 1977/78

# PETER CORMACK

Peter Cormack was one of the most naturally talented Reds of the mid seventies; sometimes surprising, invariably subtle, he was a pleasure to watch. Unlike so many midfielders, he was ready to risk losing possession to make a penetrating forward pass, often changing the pattern of play with a single touch. Bill Shankly had been a confirmed admirer since the talented Scot was capped as a teenage winger with Hibernian, but it was in the more central, constructive role Peter adopted for Nottingham Forest that the Liverpool boss saw him making the greatest impact.

After paying £110,000 to prise him away from the City Ground in the summer of 1972, Shanks introduced Peter to his Championship-chasing side at the expense of the more prosaic Brian Hall, and revelled in his success. The new man quickly showed his mettle with incisive displays in which he employed his extensive repertoire of deft skills to full advantage and demonstrated that, for all his slight build, he was no shirker in the tackle. Despite standing only 5ft 8in tall he was also good in the air – thanks to instinctive timing of the Ian St John variety – as Everton found out to their cost when he ghosted in at the near post to head the only goal of the October 1972 derby at Anfield.

Peter found a particularly able collaborator in Kevin Keegan, the quick-witted pair often dazzling opponents with their lightning one-two exchanges, and soon after the all-Mersey clash, Birmingham fell victim to their tricks in front of the Kop. The Cormack–Keegan tandem seemed to skate over the greasy, rain-soaked surface, inspiring a thrilling 4–3 win after the Reds had trailed at the interval.

Despite his undeniable artistic attributes, however, there were times when Peter's contribution could be peripheral, his abilities submerged in the hurly-burly of the game, and there were those who championed the more consistent merits of the worthy Hall. But Shankly was convinced of his values and he shared in League, FA Cup and UEFA Cup glory before a combination of cartilage trouble and the advance of other midfielders precipitated a November 1976 move to Bristol City. For three years he entertained fitfully at Ashton Gate before heading for Hibs and home.

BORN: Edinburgh, 17.7.46. GAMES: 168 (9). GOALS: 26.
HONOURS: UEFA Cup 72/3. League Championship 72/3, 75/6. FA Cup 73/4.
9 Scotland caps.

OTHER CLUBS: Hibernian; Nottingham Forest 69/70–71/2 (74, 15);
Bristol City 76/7–79/80 (67, 15); Hibernian. MANAGER: Partick Thistle;
Anartosi, Cyprus.

## 1972/73 – 1975/76

## STEVE PEPLOW 1969/70

Forward. BORN: Liverpool, 8.1.49. GAMES: 3. GOALS: 0.
OTHER CLUBS: Swindon Town 70/1–72/3 (40, 11);
Nottingham Forest 73/4 (3, 0); Mansfield Town *on loan* 73/4 (4, 3);
Tranmere Rovers 73/4–80/1 (248, 44).

## CHRIS FAGAN 1970/71

Full-back. BORN: Manchester, 5.6.50. GAMES: 1. GOALS: 0.
OTHER CLUBS: Tranmere Rovers 71/2–74/5 (84, 2).

## STEVE ARNOLD 1970/71

Midfielder/Defender. BORN: Crewe, 5.1.51. GAMES: 1.
GOALS: 0. OTHER CLUBS: Crewe Alexandra 68/9–70/1 (15, 0);
Southport *on loan* 71/2 (16, 3); Torquay United *on loan*
72/3 (3, 1); Rochdale 73/4 (40, 1).

## FRANK LANE 1972/73

Goalkeeper. BORN: Wallasey, 20.7.48. GAMES: 2. GOALS: 0.
OTHER CLUBS: Tranmere Rovers 69/70–71/2 (76, 0);
Notts County 75/6 (2, 0).

## TREVOR STORTON 1972/73—1973/74

Midfielder/Defender. BORN: Keighley, 26.11.49.
GAMES: 11 (1). GOALS: 0. OTHER CLUBS:
Tranmere Rovers 67/8–71/2 (118, 9); Chester 74/5–83/4 (396, 17).

## DEREK BROWNBILL 1973/74

Forward. BORN: Liverpool, 4.2.54. GAMES: 1. GOALS: 0.
OTHER CLUBS: Port Vale 74/5–77/8 (92, 13);
Wigan Athletic 78/9–79/80 (48, 8).

## MAX THOMPSON 1973/74—1975/76

Defender. BORN: Liverpool, 31.2.56. GAMES: 1 (1).
GOALS: 0. OTHER CLUBS: Blackpool 77/8–80/1 (99, 6);
Swansea City 81/2–82/3 (26, 2); Bournemouth 83/4 (9, 0);
Port Vale *on loan* 83/4 (2, 0).

## DAVE RYLANDS 1973/74

Defender. BORN: Liverpool, 7.3.53. GAMES: 1. GOALS: 0.
OTHER CLUBS: Hereford United 74/5–75/6 (22, 0);
Newport County *on loan* 74/5 (3, 1); Hartlepool United
*on loan* 75/6 (11, 0); Halifax Town 76/7 (5, 0).

## BRIAN KETTLE 1975/76—1976/77

Full-back. BORN: Prescot, 22.4.56. GAMES: 4. GOALS: 0.
OTHER CLUBS: Houston, USA; Wigan Athletic 80/1 (14, 1).

CHRIS FAGAN

STEVE ARNOLD

FRANK LANE

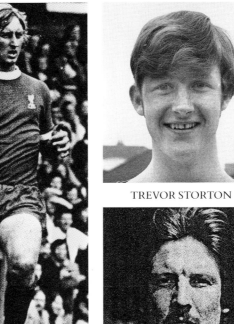

DEREK BROWNBILL

TREVOR STORTON

BRIAN KETTLE

STEVE PEPLOW

DAVE RYLANDS

MAX THOMPSON

# KEVIN KEEGAN

Kevin Keegan is one of the pivotal figures in Liverpool history and despite a dozen years of unprecedented, Dalglish-inspired dominance, he remains the biggest star the Reds have ever had. That's not to say he was the greatest footballer – such a claim would be contentious indeed – but for sheer charisma and public prominence there has been no one like him in the British game since the days of George Best.

His initial impact after arriving from Scunthorpe for £35,000 in the spring of 1971 – 'robbery with violence' was how Bill Shankly later described the deal – was overwhelming. Kevin hit Anfield like a miniature tornado; he turned the hallowed training procedures upside down with an all-consuming urge to be first at everything, excelled on a pre-season tour of Scandinavia and, having been swiftly converted from deep-lying winger to striker, found himself in the team for the First Division opener against Nottingham Forest. He scored after seven minutes, ran amok like a demented jack-in-the-box for the rest of the match and generally served notice that Shanks had finally found the elusive special additive needed to inspire his rebuilt side.

Kevin quickly proved that his grand entrance was no fluke with a series of galvanising performances which caught the imagination of media and fans alike. He was a darting, irrepressible imp of a player, scampering to all corners of his opponents' territory and not loth to forage for the ball in his own half. Quick, brave and apparently inexhaustible, he possessed a sureness of touch with both feet which enabled him to trick defenders in tight spaces and, even at 5ft 8in, carried a potent aerial threat. Kevin's most precious assets, though, were a nimble brain – a delicately drifted European Cup goal against St Etienne in 1977 was a vivid example of improvisation at speed – and almost fiendish determination, a quality greatly admired by Shanks and which did much to forge a deep bond between the two men.

Kevin, whose front-line understanding with John Toshack at times appeared to border on telepathy, was instrumental in many of the Reds' most stirring mid-seventies triumphs. Personal highlights included his two-goal show against Newcastle in the 1974 FA Cup Final and, three years later, that scintillating swansong when he ran Bertie Vogts and Borussia Moenchengladbach ragged as Liverpool won the European Cup for the first time.

Sadly, but perhaps inevitably, there was bitterness on Merseyside when Kevin announced his decision to take his talents to Europe. Having been honest enough to give a full season's notice of his intention, he endured, with commendable dignity, the cooling of the Kop's ardour and perfidious jibes about his so-called greed. It even became fashionable to question his stature in the game and there were constant, slighting references to a 'manufactured' footballer, one who had reached the top by application rather than natural talent.

How short were the memories of such mealy-mouthed critics, and how blindly they now lashed out at a man who had given no more than half a dozen below-par performances in as many years at Anfield, had captained England and was to go on to twice become European Footballer of the Year. Wherever he went, including Southampton and Newcastle in later seasons, he gave princely value for money. A Pelé or a Maradona he was not, but in his own way Kevin Keegan *was* one of the greats.

BORN: Doncaster, 14.2.51. GAMES: 321. GOALS: 100.
HONOURS: European Cup 76/7. UEFA Cup 72/3, 75/6.
League Championship 72/3, 75/6, 76/7. FA Cup 73/4. 63 England caps.

OTHER CLUBS: Scunthorpe United 68/9–70/1 (124, 18);
SV Hamburg; Southampton 80/1–81/2 (68, 37);
Newcastle United 82/3–83/4 (78, 48).

# 1971/72 — 1976/77

# RAY KENNEDY

Ray Kennedy was a rare bird, a deceptively talented individual whose inimitable contribution to one of Liverpool's most imperious sides made a nonsense of any attempt to pigeon-hole him. Glib descriptions of a powerful midfielder – which he became at Anfield after years as a successful striker with Arsenal – failed dismally to do justice to his full, subtle range of distinctive abilities.

When Bill Shankly signed Ray for £180,000 in the summer of 1974 – his last act as Reds' boss – he was rescuing a slightly overweight attacker, still eight days short of his 23rd birthday, who had seemingly lost his way after playing a crucial part in the Gunners' League and FA Cup double of 1970/71. The newcomer found himself in at the dawn of the Paisley era and, despite an irritating injury which kept him out of the season's first four League games, impressed Bob enough to oust John Toshack from his front-running role. There followed a sequence of 24 games in which Ray managed ten goals, but he then lost his place as the Welshman was recalled in a bid to find a winning blend.

The turning point, however, was not far away. Towards the end of the campaign Paisley began experimenting with the former Highbury man in a deep-lying position behind the Keegan–Toshack spearhead – and liked what he saw. By November 1975 Ray was installed on the left of midfield where he was to help Liverpool lift ten major honours in six years of almost uninterrupted triumph.

His value to the team was incalculable, his footballing qualities legion, and if he didn't quite catch the eye like a Souness or a McDermott, Ray had much to offer the connoisseur. Still not the most athletic of figures – though more streamlined than on his arrival – he had a delicate touch for such a big man; he was adept at shielding the ball, a legacy of his days as a striker, and his distribution was intelligent, swift and decisive. Like all top players who are short of pace, Ray read the game well and often changed the emphasis of an attack with a sweeping crossfield pass, but perhaps his deadliest attribute was a knack of lurking unobtrusively on the left flank before making a late run into the box to finish off a move at the far post.

In important matches he habitually spent the early minutes lying deeper than usual, doing a containing job before allowing his attacking flair to blossom as the game wore on and opponents fell victim to a false sense of security. This tendency was especially marked in European encounters, in which the England international contributed some of his most vital strikes. An 83rd-minute away goal to upset Bayern Munich in the 1981 European Cup semi-final and a fierce second-half volley to turn the tide against Bruges when the Belgians were two up in the 1976 UEFA Cup Final are just a couple that remain sharp in the memory.

Ultimately squeezed out of the side by the youthful challenge of Ronnie Whelan in December 1981, Ray joined John Toshack's colony of former Reds at Swansea for only £20,000 less than his purchase price. A brief stint at Hartlepool preceded a spell as a publican and a coaching appointment at Sunderland, before it was revealed that he had Parkinson's disease. Shanks, as usual, encapsulated the essence of a footballer better than most when he said of Ray: 'He played in no-man's land in a world of his own, but he gave the team balance. He had style and he reminded me of Matt Busby. Oh yes, Ray Kennedy was some player.'

BORN: Seaton Delaval, Northumberland, 28.7.51. GAMES: 381 (3).
GOALS: 72. HONOURS: European Cup 76/7, 77/8, 80/1. UEFA Cup 75/6.
League Championship 75/6, 76/7, 78/9, 79/80, 81/2. League Cup: 80/1.
17 England caps.
OTHER CLUBS: Arsenal 69/70–73/4 (158, 53); Swansea City 81/2–83/4 (42, 2);
Hartlepool United 83/4 (23, 3).

## 1974/75 – 1981/82

# TOMMY SMITH

If the spirit of the Anfield Reds ever took on human form it would probably tackle like a two-legged ton of bricks, bark orders in broadest Scouse and answer to the name of Tommy Smith. Here was a man, born in the shadow of his beloved ground, who served Liverpool for 18 years and grew to be the very personification of his club. He will go down in folklore as one of the hardest men the game has known – and he was – but to write him off as a mere destroyer is a mistake. Oh yes, Tommy could play a bit, too.

He made his debut at home to Birmingham in May 1963 as a deputy for injured right-half Gordon Milne, but it was in an Anfield encounter with Anderlecht in November the next year that he made his first major impact. Wearing a number ten shirt, he operated as an extra defender, confusing the Belgians as Liverpool won comfortably. Tommy instantly became an integral part of Bill Shankly's first great side, initially combative in midfield before moving into central defence where he could more easily make light of a comparative lack of pace. 'Think of yourself as Ron Yeats' right leg,' Shanks told him, and he developed into a trusty buttress of Division One's most formidable rearguard.

Tommy, a rumoured transfer target of Manchester United in his reserve days, was a confident, aggressive ball-winner whose distribution could rarely be faulted. His game, which always boasted more skill than he was given credit for, rapidly matured as he contributed vigorously to the 1965 Wembley victory over Leeds and the ensuing Championship campaign.

As the influence of better-known players waned with age, Tommy's authority grew ever more marked and he was the obvious choice to succeed Yeats as captain in March 1970. Taking over a team in the throes of transformation, he was an inspiration, constantly driving his team-mates to greater efforts – not shrinking from the task even if personally off form – and standing up for their rights in off-the-field dealings. Tommy relished the responsibility and in 1970/71 delivered some of the finest performances of his life, being pipped as Footballer of the Year by Frank McLintock and winning his sole England cap.

That season he led Liverpool to the FA Cup Final, which was lost to Arsenal, before going on to a then unique double of the Championship and the UEFA Cup in 1972/73. His days as skipper were numbered, though, and he lost the job to Emlyn Hughes following a confrontation with Bill Shankly over being dropped in November 1973. After nearly joining Stoke, Tommy returned to the side at right-back in place of the sidelined Chris Lawler and helped to ensure a steady flow of trophies until, troubled by knee problems and with the team prospering in his absence, he announced in early 1977 that retirement was imminent.

How an injury to Phil Thompson changed all that. The old warhorse found himself back in central defensive harness to win a title medal, face Manchester United in the FA Cup Final and, most stirring of all, head the goal against Borussia Moenchengladbach in Rome that effectively won Liverpool their first European Cup. Fired anew with ambition, Tommy stayed for another term and would have played in a second European Cup Final if he hadn't dropped a pick-axe on his foot.

The Reds offered him a one-year contract, while John Toshack came up with a better deal at Swansea, which he accepted. Tommy, who was to make a brief Anfield return as a coach, left in the knowledge that no one had ever fought more fiercely in the Liverpool cause. As one ex-opponent, himself no six-stone weakling, put it: 'There's a lot of very hard men – and then there's Tommy Smith!'

BORN: Liverpool, 5.4.45. GAMES: 632 (1). GOALS: 48.
HONOURS: European Cup 76/7. UEFA Cup 72/3, 75/6.
League Championship 65/6, 72/3, 75/6, 76/7. FA Cup 64/5, 73/4. 1 England cap.
OTHER CLUBS: Swansea City 78/9 (36, 2).

# 1962/63 — 1977/78

# PHIL NEAL

Phil Neal will take his place in soccer history as the man who combined two of the game's most priceless commodities – success and consistency – to a hitherto unknown degree. In the nine seasons between 1975/76 and 1983/84 it took Liverpool 538 games to win 16 major honours; Phil was absent from the starting line-up just four times. His haul of medals is rivalled only by that of Alan Hansen, who missed more matches through injury and needed a little longer – without actually dragging his feet! – to assemble his collection.

A large slice of the credit for Phil's phenomenal record must go to Bob Paisley, who made the full-back his first signing when he handed Northampton Town a cheque for £66,000 in October 1974. It wasn't a case of plucking a teenage prodigy from the League's lower reaches as, despite the occasional flicker of interest from bigger clubs, Phil's six years of endeavour for the Cobblers had hardly secured him a national reputation. In Fourth Division circles, however, he was known for his consistency . . .

After joining the Reds it wasn't long before he was given a first-team chance – as deputy left-back for the injured Alec Lindsay in a goalless derby at Goodison Park – and then came a short stint standing in for Tommy Smith on the right. Phil's calm, assured performances were enough to convince Bob of his ability and he became a fixture in the side. For 18 months he alternated between the two full-back roles before settling on the right, partnering first Joey Jones and then, more enduringly, Alan Kennedy as Liverpool continued to gratify English football's most gargantuan appetite for trophies.

Phil's attributes, though immeasurably valuable to his team's cause, were of the unspectacular variety. He was not a fearsome tackler, preferring to jockey an attacker into a corner before perhaps nudging the ball away or forcing a rash pass. An intelligent positional player, he was masterful at denying space to wingers who often had the edge on him for pace but who rarely gave him a chasing – Leeds' Eddie Gray was one man who very occasionally did – and he was strong enough in the air to be an emergency centre-half.

Excellent though Phil's defensive work was, the constructive side of his game was even more outstanding. His distribution was immaculate, whether playing the ball in neat triangles with his midfielders or finding the front-men with long, fluent passes down the inside-right channel, and he was adept at stealing forward to deliver crisp crosses. The majority of his goals came from spot-kicks – his most famous sealed the 1977 European Cup Final victory over Borussia Moenchengladbach – but there were also several vital run-of-play strikes, the most notable being the prod which set Joe Fagan's side on the way to triumph in another European Cup Final, against Roma in 1984.

Dependable under pressure and an on-field talker who was constantly cajoling colleagues to greater efforts, Phil was well suited to succeed Graeme Souness as skipper for 1984/85 and carried the responsibility impressively. At 33, however, he was never going to be a long-term leader and half-way through the following season he left to become player-manager of Bolton Wanderers. The achievements of Phil Neal, the most-capped England right-back of all time, will stand forever as a monument to dedication, fitness and not a little skill.

BORN: Irchester, Northamptonshire, 29.2.51. GAMES: 633 (2). GOALS: 60.
HONOURS: European Cup 76/7, 77/8, 80/1, 83/4. UEFA Cup 75/6.
League Championship 75/6, 76/7, 78/9, 79/80, 81/2, 82/3, 83/4, 85/6.
League Cup 80/1, 81/2, 82/3, 83/4. 50 England caps.

OTHER CLUBS: Northampton Town 68/9–74/5 (186, 29);
Bolton Wanderers 85/6– (64, 3). MANAGER: Bolton Wanderers.

## 1974/75 – 1985/86

# JOEY JONES

Who ate the Frogs' legs, made the Swiss roll and topped the lot by munching Gladbach? None other than Joey Jones, of course, that tattooed tiger of a left-back taken to the hearts of Kopites like few of their heroes before or since. Joey, as proud to wear the red of Liverpool as that of his beloved Wales, enjoyed an affectionate rapport with the fans, who loved his zealous approach, and they coined the colourful catchphrase to immortalise his spirited displays against the French, Swiss and West German champions on the way to lifting the 1977 European Cup.

Joey moved to Anfield from Wrexham for £110,000 in July 1975 to replace out-of-form Alec Lindsay but early displays indicated too many rough edges for the top flight. Phil Neal switched to left-back, Tommy Smith came in on the right and Joey was out. That disappointment, however, was merely a prelude to his finest season; 1976/77 saw him claim a regular place in the side which took Europe's top prize, retained the Championship and narrowly lost the FA Cup Final to Manchester United.

Throughout that glorious campaign Joey played as though his life depended on it. Possessed with boundless enthusiasm, he was strong in the air and formidable in the tackle, though there was occasionally a tendency to commit himself to reckless challenges. Unfortunately, there were more serious weaknesses; his distribution was often wayward and offered a sorry comparison to the silky skill of Lindsay, and his reading of the game was at times rudimentary. Thus it was no real surprise when Joey lost his place during the following term as Bob Paisley shuffled the Reds' defence to accommodate the increasingly impressive Alan Hansen.

In September 1978 he returned to Wrexham for a paltry £20,000 but his days in the big time were not yet over. John Neal, his former boss at the Racecourse Ground, took him to Chelsea where he was adored by the Shed as he had once been doted on by the Kop, and Joey helped the Pensioners win promotion to the First Division. There was a brief spell at Huddersfield before a third stint with his first club; this time the doughty Welsh warrior was home for good.

BORN: Llandudno, 4.3.55. GAMES: 97. GOALS: 3.
HONOURS: European Cup 76/7. League Championship 75/6, 76/7.
72 Wales caps.
OTHER CLUBS: Wrexham 72/3–74/5 (98, 2) and 78/9–82/3 (146, 6);
Chelsea 82/3–84/5 (78, 2); Huddersfield Town 85/6–86/7 (68, 3);
Wrexham 87/8– (100, 9).

# 1975/76 — 1977/78

# JIMMY CASE

It's a rare player who reaches his peak *after* leaving Liverpool but Jimmy Case is, after all, no ordinary performer. He bade farewell to the Reds at the age of 27, gave three and a half years' commendable but hardly remarkable service to Brighton, and then bloomed luxuriantly for Southampton in the play-maker's role denied to him at Anfield by the majesty of Graeme Souness. Was he allowed to leave Merseyside too soon or was the change as good as a rest? The question will always hang over the Case career but should not be allowed to detract from six seasons of stirring achievements under Bob Paisley.

Jimmy, a £500 capture from non-League South Liverpool, made his debut at Anfield against Queen's Park Rangers in April 1975 in an attacking role wide on the right, but it was not until seven months later that his explosive talents earned a settled run in the team at the expense of midfielder Brian Hall. He marked his new stature with a rousing hat-trick in 15 degrees of frost against Slask Wroclaw of Poland in the UEFA Cup and then, having also scored against Dynamo Dresden in the quarter-final, exerted a crucial influence on the home leg of the final against FC Bruges. He had been omitted from the starting line-up in favour of David Fairclough but, with the Reds two down, was called on as substitute for John Toshack and immediately galvanised the side into three-goal retaliation. Rampaging ferociously down the right flank, Jimmy unsettled the hitherto calm Belgian defence, creating several clear-cut chances and chipping in with the equaliser himself.

Liverpool's vibrant, baby-faced rookie finished his first senior campaign with title and UEFA Cup medals and was clearly a prospect of prodigious potential. His value was twofold: in attack his pace, thrust and howitzer-style shooting offered a savage threat, while in deeper positions his lusty tackling, crisp distribution and general full-blooded vitality were a productive combination. Yet despite such an impressive array of assets, Jimmy's place in the side during the treble-hunting campaign which followed was not a formality. Until the spring of 1977, when he slotted in on the right of Terry McDermott, the two had fought a well-matched battle for the number eight shirt. Come the run-in, Jimmy was on his mettle, playing an enterprising part in the League and European Cup triumphs and winning plaudits as the Reds' best player in the FA Cup Final against Manchester United. Though a Wembley loser, he had the consolation of scoring the game's finest goal, swivelling on the 18-yard line to beat Alex Stepney with a sweetly-struck half-volley.

Over the next three seasons his name was seldom missing from Liverpool's team-sheet and with Souness, McDermott and Ray Kennedy he formed one of the world's most effective – and attractive – midfield units. But in 1980/81 Jimmy was ousted by the industrious Sammy Lee and spent most of his time on the substitute's bench, clearly an unacceptable situation for a young man of his calibre.

With no likelihood of a swift recall, he was sold to Brighton for £350,000 and, in his second season with the Seagulls, had the huge satisfaction of returning to Anfield to score the goal which knocked his former team-mates out of the FA Cup. When, aged 30, he moved to the Dell for a token £25,000, Jimmy's career looked to be petering out; six years and nearly 200 League matches later he was playing better than ever, maturity having revealed unsuspected depths of craft and insight. As his manager Chris Nicholl has put it: 'If the game is a language, then Jimmy is undoubtedly a professor.' And the Case history is not over yet . . .

BORN: Liverpool, 18.5.54. GAMES: 236 (25). GOALS: 45.
HONOURS: European Cup 76/7, 77/8, 80/1. UEFA Cup 75/6.
League Championship 75/6, 76/7, 78/9, 79/80. League Cup: 80/1.

OTHER CLUBS: Brighton and Hove Albion 81/2–84/5 (127, 10);
Southampton 84/5– (190, 9).

# 1974/75 — 1980/81

# TERRY McDERMOTT

There were suspicions during Terry McDermott's early days at Anfield that he was destined to be a £170,000 misfit; he became instead a creative inspiration in one of the Reds' most exhilarating combinations. At his irresistible best he was the free spirit in a beautifully balanced midfield quartet led by anchor man Graeme Souness with Jimmy Case on the right flank and Ray Kennedy on the left. Terry's roving commission gave full rein to a potent cocktail of vision and stamina which prised open many of the world's tightest defences.

It was not always thus. Bob Paisley signed the Liverpool-born schemer from Newcastle in November 1974 after he had impressed against his home-town club in that year's FA Cup Final. Terry went straight into the side but failed to settle as the new manager experimented in an attempt to emulate the success of the Shankly era. When the trophies started rolling in, largely without Terry's assistance – Bob's Reds won the Championship and UEFA Cup in 1975/76 – it seemed likely that he would be written off as a mistake, albeit an expensive one, and unloaded.

But Paisley kept faith with the wiry ex-Magpie and when, in the following campaign, Liverpool were pushing for a squad-sapping treble, Terry began to blossom. After vying for a place with Case – whose stern tackling he could never remotely emulate – for most of the season, he became established in the spring and played a memorable part in a tumultuous run-in which saw the title and the European Cup end up at Anfield but the FA Cup slip away to Old Trafford. He was especially dangerous when running from deep positions and was adept at arriving late in the penalty area where his finishing, by turns powerful and subtle, could be deadly. Terry's most valuable goal that term – and of his career, come to that – was the opener against Borussia Moenchengladbach in Rome, where the Reds gloriously lifted Europe's top prize. He ghosted, typically, down the inside-right channel to take a pass from Steve Heighway before clinically curling the ball past the German 'keeper. A month earlier there had been an even more mouth-watering piece of opportunism when Terry had spotted Everton's David Lawson off his line and chipped an exquisite goal in the FA Cup semi-final at Maine Road.

But the McDermott zenith was not reached until the arrival of Souness in 1978. The Scot's all-pervading influence on central midfield gave the newly capped England international the liberty he needed to express his talents fully. A natural athlete, Terry made runs to all corners of the pitch, often acting as a decoy and creating space for colleagues to exploit, and when he did gain possession his instinctive control and incisive passing ability usually made the most of it.

He remained in his pomp for three years – in 1980 he was the first man to win awards from the football writers and his fellow players in the same season – and two incidents against Spurs during this period emphasised his dual value, as team man and individual. In September 1978 at Anfield he started and finished a flowing end-to-end move that capped a 7–0 annihilation, and 18 months later at White Hart Lane he decided an FA Cup quarter-final with a spontaneous flighted shot from near the corner flag.

Despite winning title and Milk Cup medals in 1981/82, Terry seemed to lose impetus and returned to Tyneside to help Kevin Keegan effect a Newcastle revival. An entertainer of class and panache had left his greatest stage.

BORN: Kirkby, 8.12.51. GAMES: 310 (12). GOALS: 75.
HONOURS: European Cup 76/7, 77/8, 80/1. League Championship 76/7, 78/9, 79/80, 81/2. League Cup 80/1, 81/2. 25 England caps.

OTHER CLUBS: Bury 69/70–72/3 (90, 8); Newcastle United 72/3–74/5 (56, 6) and 82/3–83/4 (74, 12); Cork City; Apoel, Cyprus.

# 1974/75 — 1982/83

# DAVID FAIRCLOUGH

It was not a palatable circumstance for a young, ambitious striker to stomach, but David Fairclough was invariably at his most effective in a number 12 shirt. He loathed the much-touted 'Supersub' tag, feeling it implied an inability to create a major impact over 90 minutes. Sadly for David, that was the truth.

He caused his first sensation when his goals in the spring of 1976 turned the title race in Liverpool's favour. Coming on as substitute, he won the points against Burnley, Everton (after 88 minutes) and Stoke at Anfield as well as netting in games which he actually started at Carrow Road and Maine Road. Media and supporters were ecstatic; if he could cause so much havoc at the tail-end of matches, they reasoned, what on earth could he do if he were there at the kick-off?

David, also known as the 'Bionic Carrot' in reference to his flaming hair and blistering pace, elevated his reputation to yet dizzier heights a year later when he notched what was, at the time, arguably the most important goal in his club's history. Near the end of the European Cup quarter-final at Anfield, St Etienne held the advantage of an away goal; the Reds had to score or perish and on came David for John Toshack. Six minutes from time he received a pass on the left from Ray Kennedy, dribbled past three defenders and slipped the ball under the advancing 'keeper. He was practically canonised on Merseyside and Bob Paisley named him in his starting line-up with increasing frequency.

Though 1977/78 was his most successful season to date – his European Cup Final appearance was a personal highlight – it became disturbingly obvious that David was short of class. He did have an unorthodox knack of going past opponents, often stumbling clumsily and getting rebounds from their legs, and continued to snatch the odd important goal. But his overall form was patchy and over a full 90 minutes he tended to drift out of the action, seeming to lack both stamina and concentration.

As new players arrived at Anfield, David slipped out of contention, but he remained a paradox to the last – one minute displaying a gloriously unexpected touch, the next fluffing a simple pass. After leaving the Reds he failed to settle elsewhere and will go down as a man of whom the public, beguiled by heavily edited TV highlights, expected too much.

BORN: Liverpool, 5.1.57. GAMES: 88 (62). GOALS: 52.
HONOURS: European Cup 77/8. UEFA Cup 75/6.
League Championship 75/6, 76/7, 79/80.

OTHER CLUBS: Toronto Blizzard; Lucerne, Switzerland;
Norwich City 84/5 (2, 0); Oldham Athletic 85/6 (17, 1); Beveren SK, Belgium;
Tranmere Rovers 89/90– (14, 1).

# 1975/76 — 1982/83

# DAVID JOHNSON

Reputations count for nothing at Anfield, as England centre-forward David Johnson discovered when he left Ipswich Town in August 1976 to become Liverpool's first £200,000 signing. During his initial two frustrating seasons with the Reds, neither international stature nor mammoth price tag was enough to guarantee him a regular place in the team. Not that David, a chirpy, down-to-earth character, expected any favours; with characteristic grit he fought back to justify Bob Paisley's original faith, helping to assemble a prodigious collection of silverware and, for good measure, winning five further caps.

Merseyside-born David checked in at Anfield, where he had once cheered his boyhood idols Roger Hunt and Ian St John, nine years after starting his career as an apprentice at Goodison Park. In fact, his delay in donning the red shirt would have been drastically reduced if either of Bill Shankly's bids to sign him in the early seventies had paid off, but first Everton's Harry Catterick – who was adamant that no player of his would join the Blues' greatest rivals – and then Ipswich boss Bobby Robson, rebuffed all overtures.

Having got their man at the third attempt, Liverpool pitched him straight into first-team action. There seemed no reason why David would not be a hit; he was quick, skilful and unselfish, and his courageous approach – utterly refusing to be intimidated by the most physical of opponents – was guaranteed to endear him instantly to the Kop. But the manager was blessed with a large and gifted squad and, in the course of his permutations, David was often the man to be left out. Not helped by a succession of niggling injuries, he managed only glimpses of his best form and, although he collected a title medal and figured in the Wembley defeat by Manchester United, he missed out on European Cup glory.

In 1977/78, with Keegan gone and Toshack soon to depart, it was hoped that a link with newcomer Kenny Dalglish would give the Johnson career renewed impetus, but David Fairclough was often chosen to play alongside the Scot and it was not until the spring that the ex-Ipswich striker began to look like his old self. Then came bitter disappointment – with the European Cup campaign reaching a climax David strained knee ligaments and was sidelined for the rest of the season. After beating FC Bruges in the final, sympathetic team-mates – who knew him as 'Doc' because his kitbag contained a remedy for most ailments – procured him a special medal from FIFA, but it was an unfulfilled, if typically determined David Johnson who prepared for 1978/79.

At last, however, his luck had changed. Given the luxury of two settled stints in harness, he now struck up a prosperous partnership with Kenny which was to form the spearhead of one of the great Liverpool sides. After his lacklustre interlude, David was a revelation; his sharp control, work-rate and knack of taking up good positions brought him 37 goals in 63 starts over two League campaigns, and his comeback was fittingly crowned when he netted twice against Aston Villa at Anfield in May 1980 to seal a second successive Championship.

His scoring rate diminished in the following term and when a young fellow called Ian Rush came along, David returned to his first club for £100,000. As the only man to score a derby winner for both Everton and Liverpool, he occupies a unique place in Merseyside folklore. But Anfield saw more of his prime than Goodison and it is as a Red – a title he wore with such pride – that Johnno will be best remembered.

BORN: Liverpool, 23.10.51. GAMES: 174 (30). GOALS: 78.
HONOURS: European Cup 80/1. League Championship 76/7, 78/9, 79/80, 81/2. 8 England caps.

OTHER CLUBS: Everton 70/1–72/3 (50, 11); Ipswich Town 72/3–75/6 (137, 35); Everton 82/3–83/4 (40, 4); Barnsley *on loan* 83/4 (4, 1); Manchester City 83/4 (6, 1); Tulsa Roughnecks; Preston North End 84/5 (24, 3).

## 1976/77 — 1981/82

# SAMMY LEE

Scouser Sammy Lee was the chunky bundle of energy whose skill and enthusiasm cut short the Reds career of Jimmy Case in its prime – only for his own Liverpool days to end in a similarly premature fashion. Sammy made his League debut as a substitute against Leicester City at Anfield in April 1978, scoring in a 3–2 victory, but was then stranded on the fringe of the side for the next two years. With such formidable opposition for a place – if Case seemed hard to dislodge it was hardly conceivable that he would oust Souness or McDermott – his future seemed cloudy. Youngsters in that situation often fail to make the breakthrough, but Sammy was made of stern stuff and in 1980/81 he displaced Jimmy on the right side of midfield.

A buzzing support player and relentless marker, he quickly endeared himself to the fans with his never-say-die approach – on the Kop they reckoned the young Lee had the Liver Bird engraved on his heart – and became a fixture in the team that won three successive Championships, two European Cups and four League/ Milk Cups. In some respects Sammy's play was reminiscent of Ian Callaghan's; he was a smooth passer, read the game well and had the ability to go past an opponent, though he lacked Cally's acceleration. His tackling, however, was fiercer than that of the great Anfield clubman and he often provided cover when full-back Phil Neal ventured forward. One of Sammy's most valuable defensive contributions came against Roma in the 1984 European Cup Final as the Reds withstood periods of pressure before going on to win on penalties.

At the opposite end of the pitch his strike-rate was disappointing, especially as he possessed a strong shot – as demonstrated with a goal from a powerful free kick on his England debut against Greece – and the fine touch to deliver the most tantalising of chips. But finding the net had never been his priority, and at the outset of 1984/85 Sammy Lee seemed set for many more seasons at the top; he was only 25, at the peak of his powers and an established international.

Sadly, it wasn't to be. Fitness problems and a loss of form conspired to shatter his confidence and, faced with exuberant challenges from the likes of Craig Johnston and Steve Nicol, he gradually faded out of contention. In August 1986 he left his beloved Merseyside for Queen's Park Rangers, but failed to settle and a year later headed for the sun with Osasuna of Spain. Sammy, the last local lad to rise through the Liverpool ranks to international status, performed creditably in the Spanish League but in January 1990 returned to England and signed an 18-month contract with Southampton. At the Dell he linked up again with Jimmy Case who, doubtless recalling the manner of his exit from Anfield nearly a decade earlier, might be excused for wondering whether lightning really does strike twice . . .

BORN: Liverpool, 7.2.59. GAMES: 279 (7). GOALS: 19.
HONOURS: European Cup 80/1, 83/4. League Championship 81/2, 82/3, 83/4, 85/6. League Cup 80/1, 81/2, 82/3, 83/4. 14 England caps.
OTHER CLUBS: Queen's Park Rangers 86/7 (30, 0); Osasuna, Spain; Southampton 89/90– (2, 0).

# 1977/78 – 1985/86

# GRAEME SOUNESS

There can hardly have been a more all-pervading influence in the middle of a football field than that of Graeme Souness; in his pomp he was the emperor of Anfield, a dead-eyed dictator of all that came his way. He was one of the few British players of the eighties to merit world-class status, but perhaps the greatest tribute to the lethal Souness combination of the devastatingly skilful and the crunchingly physical is that when he left for Italy in 1984 he was actually *missed*. When the likes of Kevin Keegan and Ian Rush moved on, and even when Kenny Dalglish forsook the red shirt for the manager's tracksuit, Liverpool merely shuffled the pack, changed gear and carried on with the business of winning trophies; the Scottish international play-maker's departure, however, left a void which took a full season to fill.

Few would have predicted such an illustrious career for the 17-year-old rookie when, after signing for Spurs as an outstanding schoolboy, he failed to settle in the south and left for Middlesbrough without making the White Hart Lane first team. At Ayrsome Park he began to realise his potential and looked every inch a star of the future just waiting for a wider stage. That stage, of course, was Anfield and immediately after Bob Paisley signed him in January 1978 for £352,000 – then a record deal between Football League clubs – Graeme began to hint at the riches to come. In his Reds debut at West Bromwich he scarcely misplaced a pass and quickly settled in to become the hub of a midfield which already contained McDermott, Case and Kennedy.

Graeme's first taste of glory with his new club came four months after his arrival when his incisive through-ball laid on the winner for Dalglish in the European Cup Final against FC Bruges. In the campaigns which followed, his dominance mushroomed as he orchestrated some of the most compelling football ever served up by a Liverpool side, spearing passes to all corners of the pitch and tackling with an implacable ferocity which at times bordered on the brutal. Tottenham felt the Souness bite in March 1982 when he came on as substitute – he was returning after a back injury – with the Reds two goals down in a match thus far dominated by the strength of Graham Roberts and company. The abrasive number 12 soon made his mark, and the final score was 2–2. Graeme supplemented his creative and ball-winning talents with occasional displays of potent finishing, none more emphatic than the thunderous volley which screamed past Paddy Roche into the Manchester United net at Anfield in February 1978, nor more valuable than the swivelling drive which beat Everton in the 1984 Milk Cup Final replay.

Was Graeme the complete player? Well, he lacked pace, though the side's pattern of play rendered the defect irrelevant, and for a man standing only an inch short of six feet he was poor in the air. But such a trifle paled into nothingness compared with his overall contribution which, after a wretched team showing at home to Manchester City on Boxing Day 1981, increased still further when he replaced Phil Thompson as captain. In his 29 months in charge Graeme led Liverpool to three successive League titles and League/Milk Cups and one European Cup to become the most successful skipper in the club's history, forcibly demanding – and usually getting – the highest standards. In June 1984 he made a £650,000 move to Italy, where his brand of play was well suited, and he prospered there for two years before returning to Britain to have an even more significant effect on Glasgow Rangers than he had exerted on Liverpool. Graeme Souness – a man held more in awe than affection by most fans – was once again stamping his authority on one of football's greatest institutions.

BORN: Edinburgh, 6.5.53. GAMES: 350 (2). GOALS: 56.
HONOURS: European Cup 77/8, 80/1, 83/4. League Championship 78/9, 79/80, 81/2, 82/3, 83/4. League Cup 80/1, 81/2, 82/3, 83/4. 54 Scotland caps.

OTHER CLUBS: Middlesbrough 72/3–77/8 (176, 22); Sampdoria; Glasgow Rangers. MANAGER: Glasgow Rangers.

# 1977/78 — 1983/84

# ALAN HANSEN

Alan Hansen is not a flamboyant man. If he were, if his football exuded fire instead of ice, and he greeted triumph with a swagger rather than his customary unassuming shrug, he would certainly have received a more generous measure of the public acclaim which is his inalienable due as the outstanding British defender of the last decade. But no matter if his immaculate skills have rarely earned the tabloid headlines. Alan can be content that no one in the game – with the mysterious exception of successive Scottish team managers – has undervalued his colossal contribution to 13 seasons of almost uninterrupted Anfield glory as he ploughed his elegant furrow at the heart of the Reds defence.

The £100,000 signing of the tall, spindly centre-back from Partick Thistle in May 1977 was arguably Bob Paisley's most canny excursion into the transfer market. In the subsequent campaign, a handful of appearances deputising for the injured Phil Thompson made it amply clear that the pale, dark-haired youngster was an inspired long-term investment, even if the characteristic calm that was later to be hailed as one of his supreme assets set off tremors of apprehension on the Kop. Fans not familiar with the Hansen trademark of unflappability under pressure would gape as an apparently casual Alan would dribble his way out of the most perilous situation. Occasionally he would be caught in possession but, his confidence increasing as he replaced Emlyn Hughes as Thompson's regular partner in 1978/79, such errors grew so infrequent as to become collectors' items.

As the eighties dawned, Alan matured into a well-nigh matchless performer, his cool approach becoming ever more a speciality as the years went by. Indeed, today, if he finds touch it is construed as wild panic! An instinctive ability to read the game provides the platform for his more obvious skills and offsets a distinct lack of pace which has been shown up only rarely – Gary Lineker *did* manage it in the first half of the 1986 FA Cup Final. Having won the ball, probably by an intelligent interception, Alan invariably makes the time and space to use it effectively, usually laying it off with the utmost precision. Rarely has a defender been blessed with silkier distribution – the chipped pass which tore open the Manchester United defence and enabled Steve McMahon to set up a John Aldridge goal at Old Trafford in November 1987 would have done credit to any play-maker. Alternatively he might embark on one of those imperious sallies deep into opposition territory, with all the dignity – even majesty – of a ship in full sail, offering the side an extra attacking dimension.

Of course, the more mundane tasks are not beyond Alan. He is efficient in both the air and the tackle, though his economical, unobtrusive style means that he seldom seems stretched, and it's certainly unusual for him to land on his backside. An even temperament – Joe Jordan, in the 1979 FA Cup semi-final, was one of the few men to rattle him – made him an ideal choice to replace Phil Neal as captain in October 1985 and his leadership played a vital part in that season's League/FA Cup double.

Throughout an Anfield career which has seen Alan thrive in successive partnerships with Thompson, Mark Lawrenson, Gary Gillespie and Glenn Hysen and brought him 16 major honours to date, Alan has often suffered knee trouble, but it was not until 1988/89 that he endured a lengthy lay-off. Now 35, Alan's playing future must necessarily be limited. If Kenny Dalglish can find a replacement of comparable excellence then he will have achieved, not for the first time, a soccer miracle.

BORN: Alloa, 13.6.55. GAMES: 604 (4). GOALS: 13.
HONOURS: European Cup 77/8, 80/1, 83/4. League Championship 78/9, 79/80, 81/2, 82/3, 83/4, 85/6, 87/8, 89/90. FA Cup 85/6, 88/9. League Cup 80/1, 82/3, 83/4. 26 Scotland caps.

OTHER CLUBS: Partick Thistle.

# 1977/78 —

# RICHARD MONEY

When Liverpool paid Fulham £300,000 for England B and under-21 international Richard Money and promptly installed him in the reserves, it was no surprise to seasoned Anfield-watchers. It seemed inevitable that the Reds had signed up another promising youngster who would serve his time in the Central League before emerging a top-grade performer as the likes of Ray Clemence, Larry Lloyd and Alan Hansen had done before him. Sadly for Richard, the system is not infallible.

In his first term as a Red he made reasonable progress, twice deputising in the centre of defence – his favoured position – for Alan Hansen and even managing, briefly, to oust Alan Kennedy at left-back. A classy operator who was good in the air and comfortable on the ball, Richard hinted at a big-match temperament with sound displays in the successful second legs of two semi-finals – away to Bayern Munich in the European Cup and at home to Manchester City in the League Cup.

But Alan's resurgence in form and the arrival in August 1981 of Mark Lawrenson effectively closed the first-team door, and Richard joined Luton for £100,000. He never fulfilled his early potential and eventually returned to his first club, Scunthorpe, before becoming a coach.

BORN: Lowestoft, 13.10.55. GAMES: 15 (2). GOALS: 0.

OTHER CLUBS: Scunthorpe United 73/4–77/8 (173, 4); Fulham 77/8–79/80 (106, 3); Derby County *on loan* 81/2 (5, 0); Luton Town 81/2–82/3 (44, 1); Portsmouth 83/4–85/6 (17, 0); Scunthorpe United 85/6–88/9 (100, 0).

## 1980/81

# HOWARD GAYLE

According to the Kop, Howard Gayle was the quickest thing on two legs – and Bayern Munich would certainly not disagree. The West Germans fell victim to the young winger's blistering speed in the second leg of the 1981 European Cup semi-final when he was brought on as substitute for the injured Kenny Dalglish. The Reds, hunting an away goal to reach the final (eventually supplied by Ray Kennedy), sent on Howard to run at the Bayern defenders and his pace had them floundering. Ultimately they were reduced to fouling him and when the enthusiastic rookie showed signs of retaliating he, in turn, was replaced by Jimmy Case.

It had been a performance of raw promise but the strongly-built Merseysider could not live up to it. Skilful and possessing a strong shot, Howard excelled in the Central League where he spent four fruitful seasons, but perhaps did not have the temperament for the big time. He was also unfortunate in that Liverpool at that time operated a four-man midfield which left little scope for a winger.

After various loan spells, Howard joined Birmingham City for £75,000 in January 1983 and won England under-21 recognition during an often impressive First Division stay at St Andrews. Further travels brought limited success before he seemed to settle with Blackburn Rovers. Late in his career he had at last achieved a degree of consistency.

BORN: Liverpool, 18.5.58. GAMES: 3 (2). GOALS: 1.

OTHER CLUBS: Fulham *on loan* 79/80 (14, 0); Newcastle United *on loan* 82/3 (8, 2); Birmingham City 82/3–83/4 (46, 9); Sunderland 84/5–85/6 (48, 4); Dallas Sidekicks; Stoke City 86/7 (6, 2); Blackburn Rovers 87/8– (88, 25).

## 1980/81

# AVI COHEN

Avi Cohen was a back-four player of poise and class who had all the ability needed to make the grade with Liverpool but didn't stay long enough to do so. He stepped off the plane from Tel Aviv in May 1979 with a reputation as Israel's best all-round performer yet, at a cost of £200,000, he represented a sizeable gamble. Four months later in his first senior outing – replacing injured midfielder Ray Kennedy at Leeds – his peripheral showing proved he had plenty to learn about English football.

After six months of Reds-style training, Avi reappeared at left-back as deputy for Alan Kennedy and managed to score at both ends against Aston Villa at Anfield in the game that clinched the Championship. The second goal, the one that beat the visiting 'keeper, sent the Kop into paroxysms of delight and seemingly signalled the birth of a new hero.

Avi, as popular with team-mates as he was with the fans, complemented smooth distribution and shrewd anticipation with strength in the air and courage in the tackle, though he was a little short of pace. In 1980/81 he enjoyed an early run which threatened to evict Alan from the side but then, perhaps yearning for sunshine, he returned to Tel Aviv. Six years later he braved another British winter to be briefly reunited with former Liverpool team-mate Graeme Souness at Glasgow Rangers.

BORN: Cairo, 14.11.56. GAMES: 20 (3). GOALS: 1.
HONOURS: Israel caps.

OTHER CLUBS: Macabbi, Tel Aviv (twice); Glasgow Rangers.

## 1979/80 — 1980/81

# COLIN IRWIN

Central defender Colin Irwin suffered two unhappy endings in a brief soccer career: hot competition brought his Liverpool days to a frustrating close and then, when he was making the most of a new start at Swansea, he was cruelly forced by injury into early retirement.

Colin had been an Anfield professional for nearly five years before making his debut in August 1979 at home to West Bromwich Albion. He gave a tidy display alongside Phil Thompson and that season made 14 appearances, deputising in turn for Alan Hansen and left-back Alan Kennedy.

It was a valuable grounding for his big chance in 1980/81 when knocks to Hansen and Thompson gave him an unbroken run of 17 League matches, with bonuses of a Wembley trip for the drawn League Cup Final against West Ham and a place in the away clash with Bayern Munich which put the Reds in the European Cup Final. Strong but never quite commanding, Colin again did a steady job without revealing the class to merit a first-team future, and when John Toshack's £340,000 offer to take him to Vetch Field coincided with the arrival of Mark Lawrenson, he was allowed to leave. He captained the Swans to sixth position in the First Division before bowing out, a sad casualty of soccer misfortune.

BORN: Liverpool, 9.2.57. GAMES: 40 (4). GOALS: 3.
OTHER CLUBS: Swansea City 81/2–83/4 (48, 0).

## 1979/80 — 1980/81

# KENNY DALGLISH

There were Bobby Charlton and Jimmy Greaves, Denis Law and George Best; to list the absolute cream of British forwards over the last three decades is not an arduous task. But now the playing career of Kenny Dalglish is effectively over and his achievements can be seen in true perspective, it is fitting that the name of the Scottish master be added to that exalted company. His exploits for Celtic alone would fill a book but it was the sublime gifts he displayed for Liverpool that lifted him on to the very highest plane. Kenny was one of those rare performers who brought true beauty to sport, his football at once exhilarating and aesthetic; some of his goals were acts of artistic creation and those who saw him at his peak were privileged indeed.

He arrived at Anfield from Parkhead in August 1977 for £440,000, then a record fee between British clubs, and inherited the number seven shirt from Kevin Keegan. After a quiet start against Manchester United in the Charity Shield, he marked his League debut with a goal at Middlesbrough and it soon became apparent that the Reds had made an inspired investment. Kenny's first Anfield term yielded 30 goals in 59 matches but that represented only the most obvious aspect of his value; such was his prodigious natural ability that he gave a new dimension to the team. Endowed with magnetic control and a deadly instinct for releasing the ball with nigh-perfect precision and timing, he brought the best out of team-mates, often creating for them precious extra seconds in which to capitalise on his skills. The Dalglish genius – yes, he *was* that good – was most eye-catching in crowded penalty areas. Wriggling like some muscular eel, he would feint one way, turn another and squeeze a vicious shot or exquisitely weighted pass through the narrowest of gaps.

Never a sprinter of Lineker-type velocity, Kenny's primary speed was of thought and he actually turned what would have been a defect in a lesser player – his lack of heading prowess – to his advantage. When faced with hulking defenders he would not waste time on ineffectual aerial challenges, instead looking to where the ball might drop, often as not arriving in exactly the right spot with almost uncanny anticipation. Crucially, too, Kenny had a tough streak. Solidly built with a low centre of gravity, he tackled with his whole body-weight and was strong enough to take most of the knocks which inevitably came his way, as his appearance record – he was ever-present in five of his first six League campaigns – eloquently reveals.

But rich and varied though Kenny's all-round talents were, it was his goals, so often the product of sheer virtuosity, that evoked the most wonder and created countless immortal memories: the subtle, Greaves-like dink to end the deadlock against FC Bruges in the 1978 European Cup Final; the delicate chip and curling, top-corner drive past poor Paul Cooper of Ipswich in two late-seventies League encounters; the 1981 League Cup Final winner, a delicious volley on the turn against West Ham; and the Stamford Bridge strike which secured the 1985/86 Championship, when Kenny took a Jim Beglin pass on his chest and, with characteristic calm, clipped the ball imperiously past Tony Godden. Golden moments all, though any Liverpool fan could recall another dozen equally thrilling and timeless examples of Dalglish magic.

In 1985 Kenny, the only Scot to win 100 caps, took over as the Reds' boss and by 1990 his managerial achievements were already rivalling his playing triumphs. But however extravagant any future honours prove to be, they could never outshine the on-the-field glory of the man who could justly be called the greatest footballer in Liverpool's history.

BORN: Glasgow, 4.3.51. GAMES: 481 (16). GOALS: 168.
HONOURS: European Cup 77/8, 80/1, 83/4. League Championship 78/9, 79/80, 81/2, 82/3, 83/4, 85/6. FA Cup: 85/6. League Cup: 80/1, 81/2, 82/3, 83/4. 102 Scotland caps.

OTHER CLUBS: Celtic. MANAGER: Liverpool.

# 1977/78 – 1988/89

# ALAN KENNEDY

Alan Kennedy was the buccaneering Wearsider who solved Liverpool's nagging left-back problem at the end of the seventies and went on to earn Anfield immortality by scoring the goals which won two European Cups – even if one of them, as he still emphasises with typical modesty, was in a penalty shoot-out.

Bob Paisley turned to Alan, one of the few Newcastle players to impress against the Reds in the 1974 FA Cup Final, in August 1978 after deciding to replace the worthy but unpolished Joey Jones. The fee of £330,000 was considered a massive outlay for a full-back, but Alan was approaching his prime and there was every reason to believe that his game would benefit from playing alongside top-class performers.

Unlike a number of other expensive Liverpool investments, the newcomer became an instant first-team regular, catching the eye with a scorching turn of speed which amply compensated for a sporadic tendency to commit himself to challenges in forward positions. He could be beaten on the half-way line but recover to win the ball before his opponent, believing Alan to be trailing safely in his wake, could reach the Reds' penalty area. His adventurous streak – characterised by surging left-flank runs which often took him past defenders and occasionally culminated in stinging strikes on goal – combined with an uncompromising tackle and endless enthusiasm to endear him to Kopites, who affectionately dubbed him 'Barney Rubble' after the Flintstones cartoon character.

Alan was at first slightly disconcerted by the need to adapt to the Liverpool method of building attacks from the back. At St James' Park he had been accustomed to slinging long balls forward for Malcolm Macdonald and John Tudor; now he was expected to play it short to Ray Kennedy, Terry McDermott or Kenny Dalglish. His distribution, initially a little erratic, improved with experience and he eventually became especially adept at one-two combinations with Kenny.

Overall, the former Magpie clearly vindicated Paisley's decision to buy him, playing a spirited part in the Championship triumphs of his first two campaigns, and when his character was put to the test in 1980/81 it was not found wanting. He had struck an inconsistent patch of form and the manager experimented with both Richard Money and Avi Cohen, but Alan – though troubled by injuries – fought back to regain his place in time for the European Cup Final against Real Madrid, a game that was to bring the most memorable moment of his Reds career. With nine minutes left and the score tied at 0–0, Alan received a throw-in from Ray Kennedy on the left and moved into the Spaniards' half. Unmolested by a defence which presumably expected a cross, the enterprising left-back cut in to arrow the ball over the 'keeper's shoulder for the winner.

As if inspired by that supreme moment, Alan took on new stature. He came under pressure on the arrival of Mark Lawrenson but again re-established himself to take three more (consecutive) title medals, being ever-present in 1982/83 and 1983/84. Then came his decisive penalty in the 1984 European Cup sudden-death defeat of Roma and a belated England call-up – he had dropped out with injury when picked nine years earlier. When finally ousted by Jim Beglin in the autumn of 1985, Alan joined Sunderland, his home-town club, for £100,000. He could walk out of Anfield with head held high, secure in the knowledge of a job well done.

BORN: Sunderland, 31.8.54. GAMES: 347 (2). GOALS: 21.
HONOURS: European Cup 80/1, 83/4. League Championship 78/9, 79/80, 81/2, 82/3, 83/4. League Cup 80/1, 81/2, 82/3, 83/4. 2 England caps.
OTHER CLUBS: Newcastle United 72/3–77/8 (158, 9);
Sunderland 85/6–86/7 (54, 2); Hartlepool United 87/8 (5, 0); Beerschot,
Belgium; Wigan Athletic 87/8 (22, 0); Wrexham 89/90 (7, 0).

## 1978/79 – 1985/86

# PHIL THOMPSON

The wiry, almost scrawny frame of Phil Thompson was a source of much amusement to Bill Shankly. But the Reds' wisecracking boss knew an outstanding player when he saw one and his quips about 'the matchstick man with sparrow's legs' masked a profound respect and admiration for the former Kopite who lived for Liverpool. To be honest, Phil's spindly appearance hardly tied in with the popular image of a top footballer but, as most forwards of his era would testify, there wasn't a more awkward central defender to be found in the First Division – and precious few with more skill.

Originally a midfielder, Phil made his debut as a substitute at Old Trafford in April 1972 and went on to squeeze in just enough appearances in assorted positions to qualify for a Championship medal in the following season. He impressed with precise passing and improbably fierce tackling but was often found wanting for pace, and it became clear that his prospects in his chosen role were strictly limited. Shankly, however, had spotted a rich vein of potential, and when centre-half Larry Lloyd was injured in February 1974, it was to Phil that the manager turned to partner Emlyn Hughes in the middle of his back four.

The enthusiastic Scouser was a natural in his new role. Though not as aerially dominant as his predecessor, he was an exquisite reader of the game who brought new modus operandi to the Reds' defence. Whereas in the days of Yeats and Lloyd towering headers were often the preferred option for clearances, Phil was more likely to play his way out of trouble in European style, retaining possession and setting up attacks with his neat distribution.

One of the first to experience his cool, ruthless efficiency was Newcastle United's garrulous centre-forward Malcolm Macdonald, who had imprudently trumpeted to the world how he was going to bring Liverpool to their knees at Wembley in 1974. In the event it was Malcolm who partook of humble pie, as Phil blotted him out of what proved to be the most one-sided FA Cup Final for years.

The Hughes–Thompson combination steadily grew in authority, remaining at the heart of the Reds' rearguard as the trophies piled up throughout the second half of the seventies. It was ultimately broken in 1978/79 when Emlyn relinquished his place to Alan Hansen and the captaincy went to Phil, who proved an inspiring and highly vocal motivator. The new pairing prospered, with the Scot's sophisticated, often adventurous style dovetailing comfortably with his skipper's more simple but equally effective approach. When Liverpool were pouring forward en masse it was invariably Phil who held his position at the back, ready to deal with breakaway threats, and few British defenders were more accomplished in one-on-one encounters.

Liverpool's success did not abate during his spell in charge. He led his side to two League titles and 1981 European Cup victory over Real Madrid, making up for missing the 1977 final through injury, before Graeme Souness took the reins in 1981/82. Phil, who had a short stint as England skipper during a distinguished international career, went on to win two more Championship medals and retained his Reds place until injuries and the excellence of Mark Lawrenson accelerated his demise. After 18 months with Sheffield United he returned to Anfield as a coach; one of Liverpool's most loyal sons had come home.

BORN: Liverpool, 21.1.54. GAMES: 459 (7). GOALS: 12.
HONOURS: European Cup 77/8, 80/1. UEFA Cup 75/6. League Championship 72/3, 75/6, 76/7, 78/9, 79/80, 81/2, 82/3. FA Cup 73/4. League Cup 80/1, 81/2. 42 England caps.

OTHER CLUBS: Sheffield United 84/5–85/6 (37, 0).

# 1971/72 — 1982/83

# CRAIG JOHNSTON

Craig Johnston was an Anfield enigma from first to last. He arrived in a whirlwind of raw energy and ebullience, threatening to turn the place upside down in the manner of Kevin Keegan; it didn't happen, but he stayed to win nine major honours in seven seasons – despite rarely being assured of a first-team place – and make his name as the most untypical Liverpool player of modern times. Finally, forever his own man, he effectively tore up his contract and walked out on the Reds to start a new life in Australia.

Bob Paisley paid Middlesbrough £575,000 for the South African-born attacking midfielder in the summer of 1981 and Craig started the new season as a substitute with high expectations. But it was not until mid March, with Liverpool just embarking on a surge that was to take them from an unaccustomed mid-table position to the title, that the effervescent newcomer ousted Terry McDermott. Raiding gleefully down the right, those long, curly, dark locks flying in his wake, Craig offered a fitful flair which was distinctly at odds with the Anfield tradition for consistency. His searing pace and exhilarating skill were a delight to behold, but often nothing would come of them; there was an all-too-frequent resemblance to a headless chicken as he disappeared into a blind alley or wasted a faultless dribble by capping it with a wayward cross.

Over the successful 1982/83 and 1983/84 campaigns, Craig – whose work-rate bore witness to his supreme fitness – was more often in the team than out of it, but both Paisley and his successor, Joe Fagan, were wary of his headstrong element. Bob, while a confirmed admirer of the overall Johnston package, aptly summed up the managerial dilemma: 'Putting Craig alongside ten men who were pacing themselves through a busy period was like throwing a firework into a box of safety matches.' As the Reds endured a disappointing season in 1984/85, Craig found himself on the fringe of the action, but Kenny Dalglish's appointment as manager the following term changed his luck and he became a regular in the side which won the League and FA Cup double. Kenny harnessed the midfielder's verve and persistence to the team effort and he became less unpredictable, more productive; one minute he would be winning the ball in his own half, the next scoring a vital goal such as the one which put Liverpool on top against Everton at Wembley.

Though Craig's name wasn't *always* on the teamsheet, a campaign of consolidation followed, and by 1987/88 he was at his peak. But Anfield security was not to be his; ironically soon after Craig's progress had been recognised by selection for an England squad, Dalglish bought Ray Houghton and the former Middlesbrough man returned to the periphery. In May 1988 he announced there was more to life than kicking a bag of wind and returned to Australia, where he had lived before moving to England, for domestic reasons. Craig became a full-time photographer and English football thus bade farewell to one of its more individual talents.

BORN: Johannesburg, 8.12.60. GAMES: 224 (36). GOALS: 39.
HONOURS: European Cup 83/4. League Championship 81/2, 82/3, 83/4, 85/6, 87/8. FA Cup 85/6. League Cup 82/3, 83/4.
OTHER CLUBS: Middlesbrough 77/8–80/1 (64, 16).

## 1981/82 — 1987/88

# MARK LAWRENSON

There was a time in the mid eighties when Mark Lawrenson looked the equal of any central defender in the world. He had the lot: speed, power, ball control, anticipation, passing ability, strength in the air. There was no discernible defect, and together with the impeccable Alan Hansen he formed what was arguably the finest middle-of-the-back-four combination in British football history.

Bob Paisley broke the Reds' transfer record when he signed Mark from Brighton for £900,000 in August 1981, beating off stiff opposition from Manchester United and Arsenal. The Lancashire-born Eire international – an Irish father qualified him to play for the Republic – was undeniably a top-class addition to the Liverpool squad but with Hansen and Phil Thompson in consistently excellent form there were those who reckoned he was an ultra-expensive luxury. Bob reasoned, however, that such pedigree performers seldom became available and were not to be missed when they did. The manager's wisdom was emphatically borne out in the seasons that followed.

In his initial term at Anfield Mark demonstrated his versatility, flitting around the teamsheet like some latter-day Paul Madeley, the former Leeds United utility man. First came a stint replacing Alan Kennedy at left-back before relief duty took him to both midfield and centre-back. The opening months of 1982/83 told a similar story before a serious injury to Thompson allowed the ex-Seagull to cement the link with Hansen, which was not seriously disturbed for more than three years.

For most of that time the Reds revelled in a dominance of the First Division unequalled since the all-conquering exploits of Arsenal half a century earlier. With Mark's influence becoming ever more majestic, they completed a hat-trick of titles in his first three campaigns, monopolised the League/Milk Cup and in 1984 defeated Roma to lift the European Cup for the fourth time, a performance in which the tall defender's multiple talents were showcased to brilliant effect. In the second half of a tense struggle between two well-matched sides, Joe Fagan's men were often pinned back as the Italians strove to end the 1–1 deadlock, but Mark, a natural ball-winner through timing rather than ferocity, was immaculate in both the tackle and his reading of the game. If Graziani or Falcao seemed on the point of breaking through, a long Lawrenson leg would invariably snake out to frustrate them, and but for the inspired work of the Reds' number four the penalty shoot-out which landed the trophy might well not have been reached.

The first hint of a split in the partnership with Hansen appeared when Mark took a knock during a 6–0 thrashing of Oxford at Anfield in March 1986. Gary Gillespie stepped in and the Eire star might have missed the Wembley win over Everton which clinched the League and FA Cup double had his deputy not fallen ill. But the blow which was to lead to the premature end of a glittering career fell a year later in the home encounter with Wimbledon, when he sustained a serious Achilles tendon injury. Despite several short-lived comebacks, Mark had lost too much pace and power to continue playing and he turned to management. No more would that gangling yet curiously graceful figure, sleeves pushed up and head rolling as he ran, patrol the Reds' back line. Club – and country – had been deprived of a true thoroughbred.

BORN: Preston, 2.6.57. GAMES: 332 (9). GOALS: 17.
HONOURS: European Cup 83/4. League Championship 81/2, 82/3, 83/4, 85/6, 87/8. FA Cup 85/6. League Cup 81/2, 82/3, 83/4. 38 Republic of Ireland caps.

OTHER CLUBS: Preston North End 74/5–76/7 (73, 2); Brighton and Hove Albion 77/8–80/1 (152, 5). MANAGER: Oxford United; Peterborough United.

# 1981/82 – 1987/88

# DAVID HODGSON

Rangy front-runner David Hodgson, a £450,000 acquisition from Middlesbrough in the summer of 1982, started his Reds career with a flourish only to fizzle out in sad anti-climax within two seasons. Playing alongside Ian Rush and Kenny Dalglish, the robust England under-21 international notched four goals in his first six games. His most impressive display came at home to Nottingham Forest in September when his willingness to chase apparently lost causes brought him two goals in a 4–3 victory. David's greatest asset was his pace and he could be particularly dangerous cutting in from the flanks. But once in a threatening position he was often betrayed by a lack of finesse and the opening would be wasted. At times he was guilty of failing to do the basic things well, and faced with competition as a wide attacker from the more skilful Craig Johnston – with the intimidating presence of Ian and Kenny closing off other avenues of advancement – he was, perhaps, destined inevitably for a short Anfield tenure.

In David's opening campaign, manager Bob Paisley gave his fellow north-easterner plenty of chances to impress. In truth, he didn't disgrace himself during an unbroken midwinter spell of 15 matches and his title medal was well earned. But in 1983/84, with Joe Fagan now in charge and Michael Robinson on the scene, his opportunities were fewer and he accepted a £125,000 move to Sunderland. There followed spells with several other clubs but David still gave little sign of fulfilling the promise which had first prompted Bob to take him from Ayrsome Park.

BORN: Gateshead, 1.11.60. GAMES: 33 (14).
GOALS: 10. HONOURS: League
Championship 82/3.

OTHER CLUBS: Middlesbrough 78/9–81/2
(125, 16); Sunderland 84/5–85/6 (40, 5);
Norwich City 86/7 (6, 1); Middlesbrough
*on loan* 86/7 (2, 0); Jerez, Spain;
Sheffield Wednesday 88/9 (11, 1).

## 1982/83 — 1983/84

# MICHAEL ROBINSON

## 1983/84 — 1984/85

Four years after a rash gamble by Malcolm Allison had threatened to blight Michael Robinson's career, Liverpool offered the honest, uncomplicated, head-down-and-run striker a second chance at the top level. Big Mal had astounded the football world by paying £756,000 to take the then unknown youngster from Preston to Manchester City during one of the wildest spending sprees in the game's history. Understandable failure at Maine Road had been followed by a steady spell with Brighton when Joe Fagan spent £200,000 to make him a Red in August 1983.

Michael was pitched straight into first-team action, forming a joint spearhead with Ian Rush as Kenny Dalglish withdrew to a deeper position, and when he went eight games without a goal the tongues of the I-told-you-so brigade were wagging avidly. But then a European Cup brace at home to BK Odense of Denmark and a cracking League hat-trick at Upton Park three games later restored his credibility, and despite losing his place as the manager tried various permutations, the burly Eire international remained in the reckoning for most of the campaign.

Though capable of the occasional artistic touch, Michael was not blessed with a wide range of delicate skills and, with commendable common sense, played to his strengths. He liked to run on to the ball rather than have it played to his feet and was often at his best when foraging on the flanks. His whole-hearted efforts were deservedly rewarded with title and European Cup medals – he came on as substitute for Dalglish in the 1984 final against Roma – but it was no surprise when, half-way through his second season at Anfield, Michael was allowed to join Queen's Park Rangers for £100,000. He had certainly proved a short-term investment but, this time round in the big league, it would be an exceedingly exacting critic who called him a flop.

BORN: Leicester, 12.7.58. GAMES: 45 (6). GOALS: 13. HONOURS: European Cup 83/4. League Championship 83/4. 23 Republic of Ireland caps.

OTHER CLUBS: Preston North End 75/6–78/9 (48, 15); Manchester City 79/80 (30, 8); Brighton and Hove Albion 80/1–82/3 (113, 37); Queen's Park Rangers 84/5–86/7 (48, 6); Osasuna, Spain.

# BRUCE GROBBELAAR

Bouquets and brickbats have rained on the head of Bruce Grobbelaar with equal intensity since that most eccentric of soccer entertainers succeeded Ray Clemence as Liverpool goalkeeper in 1981/82. Many shrewd observers claim he is the most accomplished custodian in the land and maintain that his habitual brilliance more than outweighs his well-publicised errors; others reckon that his slapstick antics and catalogue of clangers have prevented the Reds from lifting an even greater share of honours over the past nine campaigns. Another strand to the debate goes that, whatever his technical merits, football needs the Zimbabwe international for the sheer fun he brings to a game beset with problems.

Undoubtedly, that third standpoint would get short shrift from Liverpool's pragmatic management; the key surely lies in the fact that three bosses of England's most successful club have been content with Bruce's unorthodox efforts. Had Bob Paisley, Joe Fagan and Kenny Dalglish in turn not been convinced that they had the best 'keeper available, he would have been ruthlessly replaced.

Bruce arrived at Anfield in March 1981 as a £250,000 signing from Vancouver Whitecaps, and had little time to settle before being pitchforked into regular first-team action. He might have benefited from a couple of seasons as understudy to his illustrious predecessor – as Ray had himself once learnt from Tommy Lawrence – but with the England man moving to White Hart Lane that summer there was no such chance.

Reds supporters realised they were getting an unknown quantity but they were hardly prepared for the culture shock which Bruce represented. They loved the stunning saves, a product of a natural athlete's startlingly sharp reflexes, and were impressed by the way he sought to dominate his penalty area. They were not so sure, on the other hand, about the occasional flailing attempt to gather a cross which had passed way over his head or the disturbing tendency to leave his penalty area to snuff out an attack not far from the half-way line.

The acid test, however, was whether Liverpool won as many trophies with Grobbelaar as they did in the pre-Bruce days. And they certainly *did*. He was an ever-present in the five seasons between 1981/82 and 1985/86, during which the team lifted four League Championships and five major cups. Better still, the triumphs were spiced with humour, an irresistible combination to the Scouse legions. When Bruce was confronted with a penalty shoot-out at the end of the 1984 European Cup Final against Roma, he eased the tension with his famous leg-wobbling act – and, crucially, had the last laugh by finishing on the winning side. If he was pelted with coins on an away ground, as 'keepers are at times apt to be, he might pocket them to get the crowd on his side, and he was always ready with a spontaneous reaction to fans' banter.

After plentiful alarms and excursions in his early Anfield years, Bruce appeared more consistent in the mid eighties, and after winning his place back from Mike Hooper after a bout of meningitis in 1988/89, he struck an inspired vein of form as the side went unbeaten for 22 games. Perversely, 1989/90 brought a new rash of howlers and the old doubts resurfaced. But whatever their opinion of Grobbelaar the goalkeeper, no one should doubt that he takes his trade seriously; as one former team-mate remarked: 'Inside that clown is a dedicated perfectionist.' On his day that perfection is sometimes achieved; on others . . . well, at least it's never dull!

BORN: Durban, South Africa, 6.10.57. GAMES: 468. GOALS: 0.
HONOURS: European Cup 83/4. League Championship 81/2, 82/3, 83/4, 85/6, 87/8, 89/90. FA Cup 85/6, 88/9. League Cup 81/2, 82/3, 83/4. Zimbabwe caps.

OTHER CLUBS: Vancouver Whitecaps; Crewe Alexandra *on loan* 79/80 (24, 1).

## 1981/82 —

# JAN MOLBY

Few First Division managers can put their hands on their hearts and say they do not covet the talents of Jan Molby; yet the Danish international midfielder, a rare and at times captivating combination of dainty skills and bear-like strength, has become a shadowy figure on the fringe of the Anfield action.

Joe Fagan recruited him from Ajax of Amsterdam for £200,000 in August 1984 and pitched him straight into the team. The initial impression was of a sluggish, rather corpulent individual who lacked the speed to make the most of his natural ability on the ball. Jan played on for the first half of the campaign before being replaced by Kevin MacDonald, and a brief end-of-term reappearance as sweeper was not enough to prevent many critics from writing him off.

Never a man to be swayed by the media, Kenny Dalglish was of a different opinion. The new Liverpool manager installed a slightly slimmer Jan in his side for 1985/86, and his faith was quickly repaid. The Dane, having had time to adjust to the frenetic demands of the British game, exuded authority as the Reds' creative fulcrum, supplying Ian Rush in particular with a nourishing diet of exquisitely weighted through-balls. Like Souness before him, Jan laced his constructive merits with formidable power, and his dead-ball expertise – he scored nine of his 19 goals from the penalty spot – was well-nigh indispensable. His finest hour came in the FA Cup Final at Wembley, in which Liverpool were distinctly second-best to Everton until the hefty schemer began to exert his influence. First he put Rush through to level the scores at one apiece and then opened up the match with a succession of flowing crossfield passes, which ultimately led to two more goals.

Jan's Anfield future was apparently assured. Not only was he a success on the pitch, he also became a personal favourite with the fans, who delighted in his Danish–Scouse accent and general willingness to embrace the Merseyside way of life. The way ahead, however, was paved with problems. After playing well enough for a slightly below-par 'Pool in the following season, he broke his foot in training and missed most of the vintage 1987/88 campaign. Jan was back for 1988/89, deputising in defence for Alan Hansen, but soccer was forced to take a back seat as he was sentenced to three months in prison for a driving offence.

To his credit, Jan survived the trauma with dignity, returning to fight for his place. But, though still capable of artistic displays – as he showed at home to Charlton in December 1989 – the gifted Dane seemed to have lost the impetus of earlier days; the new pattern of play, with so many attacking ideas stemming from the Barnes–Beardsley axis, did not appear to suit his game. At 27, Jan still has time for new Anfield glories; at present, however, his career is standing still.

BORN: Kolding, Denmark, 4.7.63. GAMES: 147 (18). GOALS: 36.
HONOURS: League Championship 85/6, 89/90. FA Cup 85/6. Denmark caps.

OTHER CLUBS: Ajax, Amsterdam.

## 1984/85 —

# STEVE NICOL

No player is indispensable at Liverpool. Neither the departure of Rush nor the retirement of Dalglish left a vacuum which was not swiftly and successfully filled; that is the Anfield way. But if there is one current performer who might be missed more than any other, one for whom the manager might wistfully long, especially in the depths of an injury crisis, that man is Steve Nicol.

The versatile Scottish international, Footballer of the Year in 1989, has acquitted himself with distinction in every back-four and midfield position, and epitomises all that is best about the modern Reds. Enthusiastic and determined, Steve boasts a rich range of soccer assets: his touch on the ball – despite his need for size 14 boots – is sure and often subtle, his passing accurate and imaginative, his tackle firm. He is rarely found to lack power in the air or pace in a sprint, he possesses boundless stamina, and his classy finishing puts many a striker to shame.

Steve was imported to Anfield as £300,000 worth of raw teenage talent from Ayr United in October 1981. Then principally a right-back, he immediately found himself in the shadow of the consistent Phil Neal and was consigned to the reserves to complete his soccer education. If there were ever any doubts about his potential they were quickly stilled in an early Central League encounter in which he picked up the ball in his own penalty box and beat five opponents as he ran the length of the field to score the winner.

His initial outings standing in for Neal, on the infrequent occasions that the England stalwart was injured, boded well for the future. Despite his inexperience, Steve revelled in the responsibility, revealing an eagerness for the ball and the initiative to use it constructively, and it clearly could not be long before he claimed a first-team place. The breakthrough came in October 1983 when Craig Johnston was injured and Steve slotted into midfield. His 19 League appearances were enough to earn a title medal and he went on to play his part in that term's European Cup Final, coming on as substitute against Roma and volunteering to take Liverpool's first penalty in the deadlock-breaking shoot-out. He missed, but still took home a winner's medal.

The following campaign saw him cement his place, mainly at the expense of Sammy Lee, before he reverted to right-back when Neal left the club early in the League/FA Cup double campaign of 1985/86. Back in his original role, Steve was magnificent, but any chance of settling there was destroyed by groin problems which kept him out of action for two-thirds of the ensuing season. A return to full fitness saw him reach yet greater heights of form and over the next three years he gave full rein to his adaptability. A competent spell at centre-back in the absence of Alan Hansen revealed a new aspect of his talent, though the right side of midfield is perhaps his most effective niche. From that position he has the scope to be a potent attacking force and has contributed some memorable goals, notably a crisp hat-trick – including a sublime chip over the advancing 'keeper – at Newcastle in September 1987, and the sweetest of lobs against Southampton in the FA Cup in February 1990.

The sight of Steve, spiky red hair dripping with sweat and huge feet dancing over the ball, has become an inspiring and reassuring one for Reds fans over the past seven years. It would be a major shock if he failed to grace the Anfield scene well into the nineties.

BORN: Irvine, Ayrshire, 11.12.61. GAMES: 266 (13). GOALS: 41.
HONOURS: European Cup 83/4. League Championship 83/4, 85/6, 87/8, 89/90.
FA Cup 85/6, 88/9. 23 Scotland caps.

OTHER CLUBS: Ayr United.

## 1982/83 —

# PAUL WALSH

When England striker Paul Walsh left Luton for Liverpool in the close season of 1984, Reds fans drooled and rival supporters quaked. The prospect of a partnership between the waspish Walsh, then the most promising front-runner in the country, and the mighty Ian Rush seemed a breathtaking one for Kopites dreaming of ever more extravagant triumphs.

Paul, who shortly before his £700,000 move had been voted Young Player of the Year by his fellow professionals, was exquisitely equipped for the Anfield challenge. Quick, lithe and abundantly skilful, he was that increasingly rare phenomenon, a central attacker who ran at defenders and took the ball past them. In confined spaces he could turn to deadly effect, like some pencil-slim Sassenach version of Dalglish, and he possessed a rasping shot to cap his exciting approach work.

Expectations were sky-high, and Paul's early performances – while flawed by a slight inclination to over-elaborate and an occasional tendency to drift on the edge of the action – duly hinted at riches to come. After marking his home debut against West Ham with a goal after 15 seconds, the eel-like newcomer was working hard to establish an understanding with Rush when injury ruled him out for two months – and that was to set the sorry pattern for the rest of his Liverpool days. Whenever he managed to put together a run of matches, Paul would usually impress and the pundits would predict the long-awaited breakthrough; then he would be sidelined again and his impetus would be lost.

Despite such frustrations, 1984/85 saw Paul maintain his average career strike-rate of roughly one goal every three starts and in the following term, after again missing early matches, he ran into splendid early-winter form. Two goals at home to his former Luton team-mates began an almost unbroken 16-game sequence in which he netted ten times, and in the November encounter with West Bromwich Albion Paul was again at his irresistible best, setting up three and scoring one as the Kop roared its approval. There was another brilliant performance, crowned by two goals, against Watford at Vicarage Road in January 1986, before an Anfield injury a month later against Manchester United kept him out of the run-in to the League/FA Cup double.

There were similar tribulations in 1986/87, after which the advent of Peter Beardsley, John Aldridge and John Barnes relegated him to the role of perpetual substitute. Accordingly, in February 1988 Paul opted for a much-needed clean slate and accepted a £500,000 move to White Hart Lane. Roughly a third of his time at Anfield had been spent recovering from a cartilage injury, a hernia, torn ankle ligaments and a broken wrist, and he certainly deserved better fortune with Spurs. However, consistent first-team action continued to elude one of the First Division's most tantalising talents.

BORN: Plumstead, London, 1.10.62. GAMES: 85 (18). GOALS: 35.
HONOURS: League Championship 85/6. 3 England caps.

OTHER CLUBS: Charlton Athletic 79/80–81/2 (87, 24);
Luton Town 82/3–83/4 (80, 24); Tottenham Hotspur 87/8– (70, 9).

# 1984/85 — 1987/88

# KEVIN MacDONALD

There were times during Kevin MacDonald's first 18 months at Anfield when his form emitted echoes – admittedly faint but nevertheless encouraging – of that departed 'prince' of play-makers, Graeme Souness. Joe Fagan paid £400,000 for the promising midfielder, who had caught the eye as an inspiring skipper of Leicester City, in November 1984 after the Reds' early-season progress had fallen short of expectations.

The newcomer was quickly introduced into a side suffering noticeably from the absence of Souness and, though short of pace, he soon impressed with his assured distribution and wiry strength. One display in the FA Cup quarter-final at Barnsley in March 1985, when his imaginative approach work played an influential part in a 4–0 victory, was particularly accomplished and Kevin seemed poised for success.

However, the lanky Scot never quite became established and in 1985/86, with the likes of Molby and McMahon in direct competition, he slid out of the reckoning until injuries to team-mates precipitated a comeback during the run-in to the League/FA Cup double. He seized his opportunity and gave a series of enterprising performances, including an assertive contribution against Everton at Wembley.

That might have been the platform for greater things, but all hopes of consolidation were smashed when he broke his leg at Southampton in September 1986, an accident which effectively ended his Anfield career. After two operations Kevin fought back to fitness with commendable determination, but the combination of a strong squad and further injury trouble denied him a Liverpool future. After spells on loan with former club Leicester and – ironically – Souness' Glasgow Rangers, he joined Coventry on a free transfer in the summer of 1989.

BORN: Inverness, 22.12.60. GAMES: 42 (14). GOALS: 3. HONOURS: League Championship 85/6. FA Cup 85/6.

OTHER CLUBS: Leicester City 80/1–84/5 (138, 8); Leicester City *on loan* 87/8 (3, 0); Glasgow Rangers *on loan* ; Coventry City 89/90– (22, 0).

## 1984/85 — 1988/89

# JIM BEGLIN

## 1984/85 — 1987/88

All was right with Jim Beglin's world as he ran out for the Littlewoods Cup quarter-final against Everton in January 1987; the 23-year-old Eire international, who had played a telling part in the League/FA Cup double of the previous campaign, was apparently on the threshold of a long career as the Reds' left-back. He was firmly established and there seemed little likelihood of a more accomplished rival emerging to fill what had often proved a problem position at Anfield. But by the end of that fateful Goodison encounter, Jim's leg had been shattered in a tackle with Gary Stevens – and with it his Liverpool ambitions.

Jim, who cost a small fee from Shamrock Rovers in May 1983, made his Reds debut 18 months later in midfield but was not tried in his favoured role until he deputised for Alan Kennedy at the end of 1984/85, a stint which culminated in the European Cup Final at the Heysel Stadium. Alan started 1985/86 back in favour but Jim soon ousted him for good and, apart from one four-match spell, the Irishman held sway for the rest of a triumphant term. His talents typified those demanded of a modern Liverpool defender: he had close control, used the ball with precision and intelligence – it was his interception and pass to Molby which initiated Rush's equaliser against Everton in the 1986 FA Cup Final – and read the game shrewdly. In addition Jim was fast, strong in the air and effective in attack. If he had a weakness it was when an opponent cut inside him, but he was working on that when injury struck.

While his leg was mending Jim suffered the frustration of watching a succession of youngsters – Ablett, Staunton, Burrows – impress in his job and when he regained fitness the old confidence was missing. In June 1989 he took a free transfer to Leeds, with whom he may yet earn further honours. The ability is there, if only fortune smiles.

BORN: Waterford, 29.7.63. GAMES: 90. GOALS: 3. HONOURS: League Championship 85/6. FA Cup 85/6. 15 Republic of Ireland caps.

OTHER CLUBS: Shamrock Rovers; Leeds United 89/90– (19, 0); Plymouth Argyle *on loan* 89/90 (5, 0).

# JOHN WARK

There is no disguising the fact that John Wark was a disappointment at Anfield, partly through injury but also, perhaps, because his game lacked the all-round qualities needed to flourish with Liverpool.

He was signed from Ipswich Town in March 1984, three months before the much-dreaded departure of fellow Scottish midfielder Graeme Souness to Sampdoria of Italy. At Portman Road John had been a kingpin of Bobby Robson's refreshing side, scoring heavily with powerful shots and ferocious headers, and such was his reputation that Reds boss Joe Fagan was widely considered to have completed a sizeable coup in capturing the thrustful Glaswegian for £450,000.

Initial impressions were excellent as John slotted smoothly into the side, replacing Craig Johnston for the title run-in. He scored on his debut in a 2–0 win at Watford, and though there were not enough games left for him to win a medal in that campaign it seemed only a matter of time before his barrel chest would be covered in them. In the event, immediate life after Souness proved non-productive for Liverpool as they failed to lift an honour in 1984/85, but John acquitted himself with gusto, even excelling his Ipswich strike-rate with 18 League goals – highlighted by a hat-trick at West Brom and including only two penalties – in 40 games and contributing five more on the way to that ill-fated European Cup Final against Juventus at the Heysel Stadium.

Kenny Dalglish replaced Fagan for 1985/86 and, often deprived of John's services by niggling knocks, prospered without his countryman. The swarthy, moustachioed international's cup of woe finally ran over in March when he broke his leg, missing out not only on the League and FA Cup double but also Scotland's World Cup trip to Mexico. The following term presented the challenge of breaking back into the team but, though the Reds won no trophies, John managed only a handful of appearances.

A magnificent striker of the ball who was at his most dangerous arriving late in the penalty area behind the front-runners, John had little outstanding to offer if his goals dried up. He was admittedly strong in the air and firm in the tackle but his distribution sometimes lacked precision and he could match neither the vision of Molby nor the flair of Johnston. In January 1988 he rejoined Ipswich for £100,000 and gave doughty service, both in his former role and in defence. Looking back, John could count himself unlucky that his best Anfield term coincided with one of the Reds' rare barren seasons.

BORN: Glasgow, 4.8.57. GAMES: 90 (12). GOALS: 42.
HONOURS: 29 Scotland caps.

OTHER CLUBS: Ipswich Town 74/5–83/4 (296, 94) and 87/8– (89, 23).

## 1983/84 – 1986/87

# STEVE McMAHON

Steve McMahon is a winner, plain and simple. The fact is etched in every flicker of expression, every gesture, every line of his combative frame as he patrols the Reds' midfield like some hunter who knows that his prey is at his mercy and that it's only a matter of time before he claims it. Like Graeme Souness before him, he exudes ruthlessness, and again like the formidable Scot, he has the footballing qualities to fulfil his ambitions.

Liverpool-born Steve took an unorthodox road to Anfield, joining Everton from school and serving as a Goodison Park ball-boy before becoming one of the most promising Blues of the early eighties. But he was not happy on Merseyside; after rejecting Howard Kendall's offer of a new contract, he also spurned the chance to join the Reds, electing instead to make a new start with Aston Villa in May 1983. Steve failed to settle in the Midlands, and when Kenny Dalglish offered £350,000 to take him home two years later, the deal was swiftly completed. It was the first signing by Liverpool's new boss, and few have proved wiser.

Not that the blond play-maker immediately revealed the form which was to make him one of the club's most influential performers by the end of the decade. His abrasive ball-winning qualities, precise distribution and dynamic shooting – ironically his first goal for Liverpool was the winner at Goodison in September 1985 – were already in evidence, but the creative heights which transformed him into the hub of the side still lay ahead. In that first season as a Red he won a Championship medal, but vied for a place with Kevin MacDonald and missed the FA Cup Final victory against Everton. The following campaign, which brought no trophy, saw a maturing of his talents, and the through-pass which freed Ian Rush to score the opener in the Milk Cup Final clash with Arsenal was a foretaste of delights to come.

But it was not until 1987/88 – and the arrival of John Barnes and Peter Beardsley – that Steve began to realise his full potential. He was the perfect provider for the gifted newcomers and, as his confidence grew, so did his authority in the centre of midfield. Fierce tackling remained a basic part of his game, but he now revealed creativity and vision at which he had previously only hinted; his passing, both long and short, grew in control and penetration, and he carried the ball with both purpose and grace.

Though never a prolific scorer, Steve continued to contribute a significant quota of spectacular goals, possessing the enviable ability to hit his shots hard and low, a nightmarish combination for goalkeepers. Oxford United were on the receiving end of one particularly fearsome strike at the Manor Ground on Boxing Day 1987, and Manchester United's Chris Turner, rooted to his line as he was passed by a 25-yard piledriver at Anfield three months later, will also vouch for the velocity of McMahon's missiles. Power, however, does not provide his only means of finding the net, as he demonstrated with a cheeky chip in the 9–0 demolition of Crystal Palace in the autumn of 1989.

As the nineties began, Steve had broken into the England squad and had most of a five-year contract with the Reds to run. He was at his peak and still playing as though his life depended on it. Though never *quite* matching the omnipotence of Souness, he was close enough for the comparison to be made. And praise doesn't come much higher than that.

BORN: Liverpool, 20.8.61. GAMES: 213 (2). GOALS: 45.
HONOURS: League Championship 85/6, 87/8, 89/90. FA Cup 88/9.
11 England caps.

OTHER CLUBS: Everton 80/1–82/3 (100, 11); Aston Villa 83/4–85/6 (75, 7).

# 1985/86 —

# GARY ABLETT

If Gary Ablett ever harboured doubts about the paramount need for patience as he fights for a regular first-team niche at Anfield, the events of 1989/90 must have removed them unceremoniously.

Utility defender Gary, the first Liverpudlian since Sammy Lee to appear in more than a handful of matches for the Reds, had made steady progress since making his League debut at Charlton in December 1986. Deputising in both full-back berths and in the middle of the back four, he had distinguished himself with a succession of sound, composed performances.

Gaunt of build and spidery of movement, Gary was perhaps not the paciest of operators but he timed his tackles well, was solid in the air and boasted a neat line in unfussy distribution. His temperament was impeccable and, after missing only the first three League games of 1988/89, he might have been excused for feeling that he was established.

But nowhere is competition for places hotter than at Anfield. The arrival of Glenn Hysen and the rapid progress of Steve Staunton and David Burrows relegated Gary in the pecking order, and his opportunities in the new campaign were limited. Yet a measure of his standing was that when Middlesbrough offered £700,000 for him, Kenny Dalglish said no, just as Joe Fagan had four years earlier when Gary attracted a six-figure offer from Derby following a loan spell at the Baseball Ground.

Liverpool's steadfast refusal to part with Gary must give him confidence, and the England under-21 international continues to make the most of what chances come his way. He certainly impressed when standing in at centre-back – arguably his best position – in the Littlewoods Cup defeat at Highbury in October 1989, but when Hysen and Alan Hansen returned he was sidelined once more. Gary deserves better than to be a perpetual reserve and ultimately Dalglish may be faced with the dilemma – pick him or lose him.

BORN: Liverpool, 19.11.65.
GAMES: 85 (6). GOALS: 1.
HONOURS: League Championship 87/8, 89/90.
FA Cup 88/9.

OTHER CLUBS: Derby County *on loan* 84/5 (6, 0); Hull City *on loan* (86/7 (5, 0).

## 1986/87 —

# NIGEL SPACKMAN

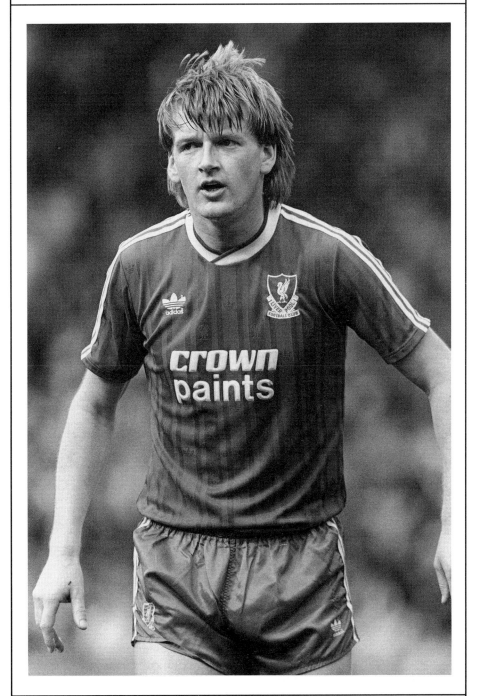

## 1986/87 — 1988/89

During the two eventful years they spent in each other's company, Nigel Spackman and Liverpool were undeniably good for each other. Kenny Dalglish parted with £400,000 to sign the tall, strong Chelsea stalwart in February 1987 when the Reds' midfield department was sorely depleted by injuries. Nigel's early performances demonstrated that while he might lack the creative skills to unlock a stubborn defence singlehandedly, there was no one more adept at doing the simple thing well. He had the underrated ability to play short passes quickly and with precision, and became a reliable foil for the more extravagant talents around him.

This was particularly evident in 1987/88 when the former Bournemouth man, who spent much of the season deputising for the injured Ronnie Whelan, was joined in the team by John Barnes and Peter Beardsley. Nigel played in more than half the matches as the Reds cruised exhilaratingly to the title, time and again proving the need for a workhorse among the artists. His stout attributes were never more sharply defined than in the much-lauded 5–0 demolition of Nottingham Forest at Anfield in April 1988 when he unselfishly laid on two of the goals for colleagues though he might have found the net himself – especially admirable as Nigel was never to score in his 63 appearances for the club.

He went on to play in the FA Cup Final against Wimbledon, but in the subsequent season a fitter squad increased the manager's options and even the versatile Nigel, who occasionally helped out in defence, found it hard to win a place. In February 1989, his job done, he left for QPR (on his way to Ibrox, as it transpired) with a Championship medal and glorious memories; Liverpool had received two years' doughty service and now picked up a £100,000 profit – splendid business for all concerned.

BORN: Romsey, Hampshire, 2.12.60.
GAMES: 50 (13). GOALS: 0.
HONOURS: League Championship 87/8.

OTHER CLUBS: Bournemouth 80/1–82/3 (119, 10); Chelsea 83/4–86/7 (141, 12); Queen's Park Rangers 88/9–89/90 (29, 1); Glasgow Rangers.

# JOHN ALDRIDGE

It was like a worthy but run-of-the-mill county cricketer taking over from prince of batsmen Viv Richards, or a rookie rider climbing into the saddle of master jockey Lester Piggott; when John Aldridge replaced Ian Rush as Liverpool centre-forward public expectations were not especially high. But Scouser John had the perfect response. He scored so freely that Ian was not missed and when the prodigal hero *did* return after a frustrating year in the Italian sun he found that reclaiming the role of the Reds' goal-scorer-in-chief was no formality. Indeed, a hefty slice of the Welshman's first campaign back at Anfield was spent on the bench as he languished in the shadow of his so-called stand-in.

John had achieved his lifetime ambition of joining Liverpool in January 1987 when, with Ian's departure in the offing, Kenny Dalglish signed him from Oxford United for £700,000. His Manor Ground strike-rate of around 1.5 goals every two games might have made him one of the most feared strikers in the land yet, strangely, there was widespread reticence in recognising his achievements. True, he had never played for a glamour club and his style was efficient rather than flashy, but that record – which included 18 months of First Division experience – would surely have made it surprising if he had failed at Anfield, instead of provoking the amazement in many quarters which followed his success.

In his first half-term as a Red, John started only two League matches but, significantly, scored in both, although it wasn't until 1987/88 that the headlines started coming his way. Even when he netted in the opening nine League matches – admittedly six of his strikes were from the penalty spot – he was accorded but a fraction of the acclaim deservedly bestowed on John Barnes. As the season wore on, however, it gradually dawned on the media that perhaps the unobtrusive front-runner who unfussily rounded off so many flowing moves should be given a share of the credit. After all, his finishing was clinical and he was better in the air than Rush; his selfless running created countless openings for Messrs Barnes and Beardsley and if John could match neither the ball skills of his team-mates nor the pace of his predecessor he made up for it with the positional sense of a born opportunist. Add to that his inbuilt passion for Liverpool – never more evident than in his utter devastation on missing his first penalty for the club in the 1988 FA Cup Final against Wimbledon – and his all-round value becomes apparent.

Despite the triumphs of his first full term at Anfield, in which he scored 26 times on the way to a title medal, it was widely predicted that he would quietly shuffle out of the limelight when Ian Rush returned for 1988/89. Once again John confounded the pundits. Ian spent most of the League opener against Charlton in the Selhurst Park dugout before replacing not Aldridge but Beardsley; John, meanwhile, was weighing in with a little matter of a hat-trick. That performance set the tone for a campaign in which 'Aldo' outscored an often unfit Ian and capped his Reds career by sweetly sweeping home the opening goal against Everton in the 1989 FA Cup Final.

Come 1989/90 it was clear that Dalglish must make a choice between the two men, and he understandably chose the one for whom he had paid more than £2 million. John, though, had one more moment of glory before going to Spain for £1 million. Just days before his September move, 'Pool were five up at home to Crystal Palace when they won a penalty and the Kop called for the Eire international. The boss betrayed evidence of a heart by calling him on, and he duly signed off with a goal; the man whom the critics had continually expected to fail had succeeded to the last.

BORN: Liverpool, 18.9.58. GAMES: 88 (15). GOALS: 61.
HONOURS: League Championship 87/8. FA Cup 88/9.
28 Republic of Ireland caps.

OTHER CLUBS: Newport County 79/80–83/4 (170, 69);
Oxford United 83/4–86/7 (114, 72); Real Sociedad.

## 1986/87 — 1989/90

# JOHN BARNES

John Barnes, as one of the most brilliant entertainers to grace British football since the war, has achieved something which has eluded every Anfield player before him: he has become *the* national symbol of the game at its most attractive.

In the same way that George Best's name was once a byword for soccer excellence, even among people who didn't know a thing about sport, so now is that of the Jamaican-born England forward. As an all-round player he does not equal Dalglish at his peak, and for sheer pop-idol appeal, he does not match Keegan. But in terms of presence and charisma John leaves the Scotsman standing, and for all Kevin's admirable qualities, he lacked the magical skills with which the former Watford winger is so plenteously endowed. Thus, without detracting from the undoubted excellence of Rush, Hansen and company, it is John Barnes, more than anyone else, who has finally bestowed upon Liverpool the glitter and panache which have traditionally been the preserve of Spurs and Manchester United.

Yet for all the plaudits which have been heaped on his close-cropped head, John was seen as something of a gamble when he headed north for £900,000 in the summer of 1987. His extravagant talents were acknowledged, but at Vicarage Road these had been tempered with inconsistency and there were fears that he was not the Anfield type.

Any misgivings, however, quickly withered as John took the breath away with a string of scintillating early performances which dazzled even the sceptics. To say he gave the Reds a new dimension is a gross understatement. A big, powerful man blessed with a sublime first touch, he was lethal when he received the ball in a deep left-flank position and ran at defences. He had the guile to gull those who stood in his way, the strength to ride tackles and a deceptive pace which took him loping away from his stricken prey. One moment John would be hemmed in by several opponents; two feints later he would be yards away, jockeying for a shooting chance. And unlike many wingers with the ability to carve out an opening, he could capitalise on his own approach work, as anyone who saw his two-goal show at home to Queen's Park Rangers in October 1987 will bear witness. One strike, a delicately arced shot past David Seaman after a captivating dribble, was a classic by any standards.

John's reward for his inspired efforts during that first Anfield campaign was a title medal and Footballer of the Year awards from fellow professionals and soccer writers alike. Understandably, much was expected of him in the 1988 European Championships, but he disappointed, as he often has in the international arena, looking more like the wayward performer who had alternately thrilled and frustrated in his Watford days. Perhaps he needs constant contact with top-class colleagues to bring the best out of him, for on his return to club duty he was as deadly as ever, only occasionally drifting through a match on the fringe of the action as if he just wasn't in the mood to play.

Some of John's most devastating displays for Liverpool have been as a central striker, and some maintain it is his most effective role. It undoubtedly affords him more freedom, extra directions in which to turn and torture his victims, who might reasonably feel that the closer he is to the touchline the less danger they are in. Certainly they have learnt that foul play within 30 yards of the goal is not the way to stop him. Apart from an even temperament which is never rattled by violence, he boasts a free-kick technique which would not have shamed Garrincha.

At the time of writing, it is being suggested that John, once more voted Footballer of the Year, may take his talents to more lucrative foreign fields. If he does, the League will be deprived of its most gifted practitioner. As for the Reds, they'll survive and prosper. They always do.

BORN: Jamaica, 7.11.63. GAMES: 135. GOALS: 58.
HONOURS: League Championship 87/8, 89/90. FA Cup 88/9. 50 England caps.
OTHER CLUBS: Watford 81/2–86/7 (233, 65).

## 1987/88 —

# PETER BEARDSLEY

Shoulders hunched and mouth habitually agape, Peter Beardsley hardly cuts an heroic figure on the field. Until, that is, the ball is at his feet. Then, suddenly, the £1.9 million Geordie looks what he is – a daring, elusive firecracker of a player, lurking with intent on the very verge of world class.

But Peter's early days at Anfield were not easy. When he moved from Newcastle United after protracted negotiations in the summer of 1987, he carried the burdensome tag of Britain's most expensive footballer. As if that were not enough of a challenge, his arrival coincided with that of John Barnes, a circumstance which both helped and hindered his efforts to make an instant impact. The England winger's sensational form deflected much of the media attention from Peter, giving him much-needed extra time to bed in, but it also set a dauntingly high standard, especially as John's transfer fee had been less than half his own.

For several months, while by no means a flop, the stocky front man failed to catch the eye and by the turn of the year had contributed only four goals. The Reds, however, remained unbeaten in the League and Kenny Dalglish pronounced himself well satisfied with Peter's progress. As 1988 dawned, the manager's faith was shown to be cannily placed, his record signing turning in a sparkling New Year's Day performance against Coventry. The former Magpie – whose route to St James' Park had taken in a frustrating one-match sojourn at Old Trafford – scored twice and had the Kop purring with pleasure at his all-round skills as he finally began to fulfil his immense potential.

That day, and for the rest of the campaign, Peter was irresistible, whether employing his speed and ball control to skip past defenders as he ran from deep positions, or slicing deadly, perfectly angled passes through a crowded penalty area. With his confidence at last sky-high, he revealed the full repertoire of tricks which had endeared him to Tyneside and, at Anfield later that month, Arsenal fell victim to a typical piece of Beardsley cheek. Nutmegging an astonished Michael Thomas, he moved forward to chip the ball over towering 'keeper John Lukic to put the match beyond the Gunners' reach.

Quick-witted and a great improviser, Peter confirmed his stature over the subsequent seasons, though he would have risen to yet greater heights if his finishing had been more consistent. Often he would appear on the edge of the box, jink past a couple of defenders and then spoil his work with a weak attempt on goal. The Beardsley boot can dispatch a devastating shot, be it blistering drive or tantalising curler, but reliable it is not.

Unlike some thrillingly gifted individuals, Peter can never be faulted for his work-rate, even if he does, now and then, seem to run out of steam. There have also been rare occasions when a game has appeared to pass him by, when he has been unable to get into the swing of the action, a fact worth mentioning only because it offers proof positive of his enormous influence. When the England striker is not at his best, Liverpool's overall performance suffers significantly, their attacking options drastically reduced by the absence of his normally incisive input. But when he is on song, which is most of the time, he continues to be the stuff of which defenders' nightmares are made. At Manchester his solitary senior appearance ended in substitution; how United must rue the day they let him go after just one hour of first-team football.

BORN: Newcastle, 18.1.61. GAMES: 127 (9). GOALS: 45.
HONOURS: League Championship 87/8. FA Cup 88/9, 89/90. 38 England caps.

OTHER CLUBS: Carlisle United 79/80–81/2 (104, 22); Vancouver Whitecaps; Manchester United 82/3 (0, 0; *Peter's one appearance was in a League Cup tie*); Vancouver Whitecaps; Newcastle United 83/4–86/7 (147, 61).

## 1987/88 –

# RAY HOUGHTON

Kenny Dalglish's ceaseless quest for perfection took Ray Houghton to Anfield in the autumn of 1987. Even at that early stage of the season, the Reds were apparently cantering away with the Championship and playing some of the most exhilarating football the First Division had seen in years. Surely the manager could not ask for more? But, of course, he could!

Craig Johnston was doing a splendid job as a right-sided attacking midfielder, but Kenny believed that Ray would be an improvement. So, after a protracted cloak-and-dagger transfer saga, he paid £825,000 for the stocky Glaswegian. Ray, who had been dumped by West Ham after one appearance and then rebuilt his career with Fulham and Oxford United, played his first match for Liverpool at home to Norwich and made an instant impact, the game finishing goalless through no fault of the newcomer. The Kop warmed to Ray as he created a series of chances with his busy runs and accurate crosses, and as the weeks went by it became clear that Dalglish had made yet another astute purchase.

The Eire international – he qualified for the Republic by virtue of an Irish father – is a tireless forager who likes to pick up the ball inside his own half and dribble it deep into opposition territory. On reaching his destination, he is less prone than Johnston to squander possession, and often startles goalkeepers with snap shots from outside the penalty area. He is also in the habit of popping up for vital close-range strikes, as he did twice with FA Cup goals in early 1988 – a header which beat Everton at Goodison and a mid-air sidefooted volley against Manchester City at Maine Road. With Ray providing a thrustful threat on the right and John Barnes casting his magic spell on the left, the Reds were superbly balanced. They were ideally equipped to rip open the most clam-like of defences, and in that glorious 1987/88 campaign, they frequently did.

Ray capped the impressive start to his Liverpool career with some enterprising performances for his adopted country, linking smoothly with clubmates John Aldridge and Ronnie Whelan in the 1988 European Championships. His dash and skill on the wider stage prompted the interest of assorted Italian clubs and huge sums were mentioned, but Dalglish understandably refused to part with his new-found gem. Ray confirmed his standing with exemplary form in the following term, being an ever-present in the team which narrowly failed to take the title and giving an outstanding display in the FA Cup Final win over Everton.

Injuries caused Ray to miss much of 1989/90, but he bounced back for the inevitably hectic climax to the season and still has plenty to offer the Anfield cause.

BORN: Glasgow, 9.1.62. GAMES: 103 (6). GOALS: 15.
HONOURS: League Championship 87/8, 89/90. FA Cup 88/9.
29 Republic of Ireland caps.

OTHER CLUBS: West Ham United 81/2 (1, 0); Fulham 82/3–85/6 (129, 16);
Oxford United 85/6–87/8 (83, 10).

## 1987/88 —

# RONNIE WHELAN

At best inspirational, at worst remarkably consistent, Ronnie Whelan has played a major part in every Liverpool triumph since 1981 – and the good news for the Reds is that the Eire international midfielder seems to get better with age.

When the sandy-haired Dubliner breezed into Bob Paisley's side in the early eighties, he made an exciting impact with spectacular goals and an infectious, ambitious style of play which, though exhilarating when Ronnie was on song, sometimes resulted in the ball being lost unnecessarily. Maturity has taught him to do the simple thing, and to do it well, with the result that he can now be counted on to perform reliably in any company, on any occasion.

When Ronnie – whose father, Ron Snr, also wore the Republic's green shirt – left Home Farm in October 1979, his destination might have been Old Trafford rather than Anfield. He had spent three summer holidays with Manchester United as a schoolboy but was allowed to slip away; the Red Devils' loss was to be Liverpool's gain and, 18 months after crossing the Irish Sea, he marked his League debut – against Stoke in front of the Kop – with a goal. It was October 1981, however, before he outstripped his countryman Kevin Sheedy, who was later to build a successful career with Everton, in the race to replace Ray Kennedy on the left side of the Reds' midfield.

In his first campaign as a regular, Ronnie could do little wrong. As well as picking up a title medal, he scored twice in the Milk Cup victory over Spurs at Wembley and received a Young Player of the Year award. To cap it all, no less a judge than Joe Mercer compared him to that great Northern Irish inside-forward of several decades earlier, Peter Doherty. Ronnie maintained his progress the following season but suffered a setback in 1983/84 when a hand injury kept him out of the side until November. On his return he seemed to have lost impetus and there were fears that he was drifting out of long-term contention, but the exit of Graeme Souness changed all that.

In the absence of the former skipper, Ronnie tightened up his game and accepted new responsibility to become a better all-round player than ever before. His distribution became more efficient, his tackling attained a keenly abrasive edge, and there was a new purpose about everything he did. As a bonus, the new Whelan retained his habit of scoring sensational goals, none more breathtaking than the first-time 25-yard curler past Gary Bailey which took the 1985 FA Cup semi-final against Manchester United into extra time.

As his medal collection burgeoned, so did his versatility. At various times he occupied all the midfield positions and effectively filled in at left-back when Jim Beglin broke his leg in early 1987. Then, in the subsequent season when costly newcomers were grabbing all the headlines, Ronnie enjoyed his best term to date. Moving into a central role to create extra space for John Barnes on the left, he was a revelation, his quickfire passing and selfless running off the ball winning new and much-deserved acclaim. His enthusiasm and level-headed approach were rewarded with the captaincy when Alan Hansen was sidelined for most of 1988/89 and he led the Reds to FA Cup triumph over Everton at Wembley.

Still only 28, yet vastly experienced, Ronnie Whelan can expect to play a crucial role as Liverpool seek to extend their dominance of English football into the nineties.

BORN: Dublin, 25.9.61. GAMES: 391 (16). GOALS: 69.
HONOURS: European Cup 83/4. League Championship 81/2, 82/3, 83/4, 85/6, 87/8, 89/90. FA Cup 85/6, 88/9. League Cup 81/2, 82/3, 83/4.
38 Republic of Ireland caps.

OTHER CLUBS: Home Farm.

## 1980/81 —

# GARY GILLESPIE

The shrewd acquisition of centre-back Gary Gillespie in July 1983 typified the meticulous planning which has helped Liverpool retain their position of supremacy in English football for so long. When new manager Joe Fagan paid Coventry City £325,000 to make Gary his first signing, it was hardly credible that the classy Scot was going to see first-team service in the foreseeable future. Joe was already blessed with the masterly combination of Alan Hansen and Mark Lawrenson, and despite five years' experience as a First Division defender, the tall, angular newcomer seemed destined to serve an Anfield 'apprenticeship' in the reserves.

Sure enough, a whole season passed in which the former midfielder and occasional full-back made but a solitary senior appearance, at home to Walsall in the Milk Cup semi-final first leg. But 1984/85 brought intermittent opportunities and Gary made the most of them; he revealed a commanding aerial presence in both penalty areas, composed and precise distribution, and a penchant for loping forward like some runaway giraffe to play slick one-two passing combinations. His campaign culminated with a promising European Cup Final display against Juventus – despite conceding the penalty which cost Liverpool the match – after coming on for the injured Lawrenson just 90 seconds into the action. Of course, all footballing considerations had already been rendered irrelevant by earlier events on that tragic Heysel night.

Gary was to get no further chance until January 1986, when he put together an impressive run – highlighted, uncharacteristically, by an Anfield hat-trick against Birmingham – and finally became established in the team. With Lawrenson sidelined once again, the former Sky Blue dovetailed seamlessly with Hansen and played enough matches to earn a title medal. Even when Mark was fit again, Gary retained his place and looked set to face Everton in the FA Cup Final, but he was laid low by a virus and missed what would have been his first Wembley date.

Over the next two terms he played some of the best football of his career, showing ever more skill and composure as his confidence grew. He was rewarded by international caps but this encouraging progress was interrupted by injuries which put him out of contention for most of 1988/89 and 1989/90. With Glenn Hysen added to the squad, Gary's prospects were suddenly not so bright, though he returned in the spring of 1990 to join the Reds' annual push for honours. If he can maintain his fitness there is still an important job at Anfield for Gary Gillespie. But, on his recent record, it's rather a big 'if'.

BORN: Bonnybridge, Stirling, 5.7.60. GAMES: 162 (7). GOALS: 14.
HONOURS: League Championship 85/6, 87/8, 89/90. 8 Scotland caps.
OTHER CLUBS: Falkirk; Coventry City 78/9–82/3 (172, 6).

## 1983/84 —

# STEVE STAUNTON

**1988/89 —**

Steve Staunton is definitely one to watch. Though still only 21, the blond Irishman has already won two major honours with the Reds and established himself in Jack Charlton's enterprising Eire side. He has the talent, the temperament and, perhaps crucially, the versatility to become an Anfield cornerstone until the turn of the century.

But he won't find it easy. Although Steve can play at left-back (currently his best position), in midfield or even up front – he helped himself to a Littlewoods Cup hat-trick when he came on as substitute for Ian Rush against Wigan in September 1989 – he is rarely sure of a place, thanks to a combination of white-hot competition and tactical switches. It can be taken as read, for now at least, that he is below the likes of Nicol and Whelan in the pecking order, and he must therefore battle for his opportunities with fellow aspirants such as Burrows and Ablett.

Nevertheless, at this stage of his development Steve is arguably the most promising of the club's youngsters. Tall and composed, he reads the game intelligently, is an assured passer and a dangerous raider down the left flank. Having infiltrated enemy lines, he can deliver a telling cross – for example, the wickedly curling effort which John Barnes nonchalantly stroked past Charlton goalkeeper Bob Bolder at Anfield in December 1989 – and if caught out of position he is quick to recover.

Steve, who joined Liverpool in August 1986 after a handful of games for League of Ireland club Dundalk, gained useful experience in a brief promotion-chasing loan spell with Second Division Bradford City eight months before his Reds debut. For the next decade, however, if he continues at his present rate of progress, Steve will have his sights set on the game's more glittering prizes.

BORN: Drogheda, Republic of Ireland, 19.1.69. GAMES: 45 (10). GOALS: 3. HONOURS: League Championship 89/90. FA Cup 88/9. 10 Republic of Ireland caps.

OTHER CLUBS: Dundalk; Bradford City *on loan* 87/8 (8, 0).

# DAVID BURROWS

## 1988/89 —

There is a certain something about David Burrows which is reminiscent of another young defender who, more than 20 years earlier, had also moved to Anfield for a sizeable fee. In similar fashion to the rookie Emlyn Hughes, David is adventurous, fiercely committed and exudes a downright hatred of being beaten. It is early days yet, but if the blond Midlander's career is half as fruitful as that of his accomplished predecessor, then the Reds will consider their £500,000 investment a wise one indeed.

Shrewd observers reckoned that Kenny Dalglish had pulled off a grand coup when he beat several other top clubs for the signature of the West Bromwich Albion full-back cum midfielder in October 1988. Though an England under-21 international, David had fewer than 50 League appearances with the Throstles to his credit, but with Liverpool in the throes of an injury crisis he found himself in immediate first-team action.

Pressed into service at both left-back and the left side of midfield, he revealed skill, strength and pace, though he was inclined to commit himself to rash tackles. His long stride made him an effective overlapper and his galloping gait was becoming a familiar sight when returning regulars and the emergence of fellow hopeful Steve Staunton edged him out.

But David is clearly a long-term prospect and, having gained vital experience in 1989/90, is now set to push his claims for a lengthy stay. Though there are still plenty of rough edges to his game, it would be a surprise if the famed Anfield coaching academy is not equal to the task of removing them.

BORN: Dudley, 25.10.68.
GAMES: 47 (9). GOALS: 0.
HONOURS: League Championship 89/90.

OTHER CLUBS: West Bromwich Albion 85/6–88/9 (46, 1).

# IAN RUSH

Every now and then, no more than once or twice in a generation, there arises in top-flight football an individual with a certain predatory instinct; no matter how exciting or beautiful the talents of more artistic performers may be, this man's special gift – the knack of scoring goals in large numbers and at regular intervals – is *the* most valuable asset in the game. In modern times, certainly since the golden days of Greaves and Law, no British player has demonstrated a more ruthless aptitude for finding the net than Ian Rush. The Welshman's record is all the more remarkable because so many of his goals have come in high-profile matches with trophies at stake, a testimony to temperament as well as supreme skill.

Yet there was a time, shortly after his £300,000 move from Chester in April 1980, that Ian looked destined to flop. In his early days at Anfield he could hardly manage to get on the Central League scoresheet, and there had even been talk of a swift transfer to less exalted surroundings. Then came a call to the colours for the 1981 League Cup Final replay against West Ham at Villa Park and, suddenly, confidence seemed to surge through the rookie striker's lean, lanky frame. Streaking down the left flank, at last revealing a glimpse of the searing pace that was to make him feared throughout the football world, the raw Flintshire lad severely tested the Hammers' defence, and though he didn't score – the nearest he came was rattling the crossbar – he gave a broad hint that the Reds' investment had not been a rash one.

But it was not until the following campaign that the real Ian Rush stood up. Then the goals began to come with a vengeance; they started with a hesitant trickle, increased to a steady flow, and over the subsequent five seasons swelled to a veritable torrent. Between 1981/82 and 1986/87 Ian hit the target nearly 200 times, averaging around two strikes every three games. Ironically, he was particularly pitiless towards Everton, whom he had supported as a boy. A year rarely passed in which Rush failed to put the Blues to the sword, the most savage execution taking place at Goodison in late 1982 when he scored four.

Ian's most obvious asset was the speed which carried him past the fleetest of defenders, but it was by no means the only weapon in his armoury. He was a clean, powerful striker of the ball and had the finely honed positional sense of all the best poachers; his first touch was usually sure and he was willing to forage for possession, though for a six-footer he was surprisingly weak in the air.

So integral was Ian to the Liverpool set-up that when it was revealed he was on his way to Juventus for £3.2 million – the deal was announced a year before he left in June 1987 – there was consternation on the Kop. In the event he was hardly missed, thanks to the Aldridge, Barnes and Beardsley triumvirate, and many observers thought the Reds were foolish to part with £2.8 million to get him back. After a year of frustration and illness, the old Rush fire needed patient rekindling and there were moments when it seemed the spark had gone. But now, with new colleagues, he was no longer playing his former role of spearhead; instead he was leading the line and often receiving the ball with his back to goal, which called for a different range of skills. Naturally it took time to adapt, but two opportunist goals which beat Everton in the 1989 FA Cup Final – one a sweetly placed shot after selling a perfect dummy to Kevin Ratcliffe and the other a delightful glancing header – signalled that his rehabilitation was complete. If further proof were needed, he struck splendid form in 1989/90, looking a more complete all-round player than ever before. All those who wrote off Ian Rush can look forward to an indigestible diet of their own fatuous words.

BORN: St Asaph, Flintshire, 20.10.61. GAMES: 387 (10). GOALS: 235.
HONOURS: European Cup 83/4. League Championship 81/2, 82/3, 83/4, 85/6, 89/90. FA Cup 85/6, 88/9. League Cup 80/1, 81/2, 82/3, 83/4.
44 Wales caps.

OTHER CLUBS: Chester 78/9–79/80 (34, 14); Juventus.

# 1980/81 – 1986/87 & 1988/89 –

# RONNY ROSENTHAL

When Ronny Rosenthal was pitched into the title race in the spring of 1990 it was like a fistful of Alka Seltzers hitting a bucket of water. Not that Liverpool were ailing – they were already firmly in pole position – but were in need of a tonic after the trauma of FA Cup semi-final defeat by Crystal Palace. Cue Ronny, an instant one-man pick-me-up. Kenny Dalglish had signed the Israeli international striker on loan from Standard Liege just minutes ahead of the transfer deadline. Ronny had recently completed a trial with Luton, who wouldn't meet the Belgians' £500,000 asking price; in view of the dashing front-runner's subsequent impact, the fee was reasonable in the extreme.

After impressing as a substitute against Southampton at Anfield, Ronny was a sensation on his first full appearance at Selhurst Park, destroying Charlton with a scintillating hat-trick. It wasn't just the goals, but the manner of them, which captivated travelling Kopites. There was one with his left foot, one with his right, and a diving header. He followed up with a sweet volley at home to Nottingham Forest and then came on as a substitute to transform a plodding Reds performance at Highbury, inspiring an equaliser with his pace and verve. It may be that with his unpredictable runaway style, he is not an easy man to play alongside. But Ronny is undeniably a performer who lifts crowds and colleagues alike, a predator of high class, as seven goals in five Liverpool starts bear eloquent witness. Wherever his long-term future lies, it promises to be a lively one.

BORN: Haifa, Israel, 4.10.63. GAMES: 5 (3). GOALS: 7.
HONOURS: 31 Israel caps.

OTHER CLUBS: Macabbi, Haifa; FC Bruges, Belgium;
Standard Liege, Belgium.

## 1989/90 —

# MIKE HOOPER

For four months in 1988/89, Mike Hooper seemed on the verge of becoming the Reds' regular goalkeeper. While Bruce Grobbelaar fought to overcome meningitis, Mike enjoyed a sequence of 24 consecutive games in which he won praise for his safe handling and quick reactions, and turned in several outstanding displays. Even when Bruce was fit, Kenny Dalglish persisted with the red-haired six-footer, and an end to the long reign of the flamboyant Zimbabwe international was suddenly conceivable. But the presence of the still-eager veteran brought added pressure, and after flapping at a couple of crosses against Sheffield Wednesday at Hillsborough in January 1989, Mike was dropped.

The former Bristol City 'keeper, a £50,000 buy from Wrexham in October 1985, had gained his first Liverpool experience in two competent spells deputising for Bruce at the beginning and end of 1986/87. His next chance came half-way through the following campaign when he returned four successive clean sheets, one of them the result of an heroic performance to keep out Stoke City at the Victoria Ground in the FA Cup third round. When Grobbelaar was reinstated after recovering from injury, Mike made it clear that, in his view, he had earned the right to continue – an attitude which demonstrated admirable confidence in his own ability.

As Bruce's junior by six years, the well-built Bristolian has plenty of time, but his next settled run in the side will provide a crucial test of his long-term aspirations. Whether he has quite the authority to fill the boots of Liverpool's current custodian is open to debate.

BORN: Bristol, 10.2.64. GAMES: 39. GOALS: 0.

OTHER CLUBS: Bristol City 84/5 (1, 0);
Wrexham 84/5–85/6 (34, 0).

## 1986/87 —

# BARRY VENISON

## 1986/87 —

Barry Venison deserves top marks for initiative. In the summer of 1986 the England under-21 international full-back felt his career was going nowhere with Sunderland, who had narrowly escaped relegation to the Third Division. It had been a second successive disappointing campaign for Barry, who in 1985 had become the youngest captain in a Wembley final when the Wearsiders had tasted Milk Cup defeat *and* dropped out of the top flight. So he wrote to Liverpool to ask if he was wanted at Anfield; the result was a £250,000 transfer and a place in the first team at the start of the new term.

He settled in with a series of composed displays, usually at right-back but occasionally switching flanks, and missed only a handful of League games. Determined and positive in his approach, Barry tackled efficiently, linked neatly with his attack and often crossed the ball well, though his overall distribution was sometimes scrappy.

He started 1987/88 as the first-choice right-back, but then injuries to Achilles tendon and calf were followed by an appendix operation and his season was in tatters. As new defenders such as Gary Ablett, Steve Staunton and David Burrows came into the reckoning, it looked as though Barry might be pushed to regain his role. The next campaign, in which he started only 14 League matches but won an FA Cup medal, proved indeterminate, but in 1989/90 he enjoyed his most settled run for three years. His use of the ball, as exemplified by the pass which cut through the Chelsea rearguard to set up a goal for Peter Beardsley at Stamford Bridge in December 1989, was improving and he was beginning to look like a long-term proposition.

Barry, a cool operator whose customary deadpan expression rarely becomes animated during even the most hectic action, may not be the most eye-catching of the current Reds, but anyone who bids to take his place will face a stern battle.

BORN: Consett, County Durham, 16.8.64.
GAMES: 111 (8). GOALS: 0.
HONOURS: League Championship 87/8, 89/90.
FA Cup 88/9.

OTHER CLUBS: Sunderland 81/2–85/6 (173, 2).

# GLENN HYSEN

Glenn Hysen cuts an imposing figure. Tall, muscular and handsome, he radiates authority and charisma – and that's before he even runs on to the pitch. When Sweden's centre-half and captain actually begins to play, the impression of power, almost majesty, is usually reinforced. He is courageous, skilful and almost audaciously calm, accustomed to aerial dominance and resourceful enough to counter most ground-level thrusts. But since he joined Liverpool from Italian club Fiorentina for £650,000 in the summer of 1989 – thus jilting Manchester United, who had expected to sign him – Glenn has not *always* found life in the English First Division to his liking.

Decidedly lacking in pace, he is vulnerable to swift interplay of passes between nippy attackers, as Southampton discovered when they punished the Reds 4–1 at The Dell in October 1989. The same defect was highlighted at Carrow Road in the following February when Glenn was sent off after resorting to two crude fouls to stop Norwich City's Robert Fleck. With the Swede playing alongside the similarly stately Alan Hansen, such an occasional problem was perhaps predictable, though in all fairness it is extremely rare for the duo to get a chasing.

Other forwards who have troubled the Anfield newcomer are Tony Cascarino, who showed that Glenn is not invincible in the air when the Reds met Millwall at The Den in November 1989, and Nigel Jemson of Nottingham Forest, whose trickery in the City Ground mud on New Year's Day often had his experienced international opponent floundering.

For all that, the Hysen presence at the heart of the Liverpool defence has generally been a reassuring one and he has given more impressive displays than indifferent ones. He is certainly a man to have on your side when the heat of battle reaches its peak, as he proved in two 1989/90 League confrontations with Mark Hughes of Manchester United. The combative Welshman put Glenn's resolve and ability to the most searching of tests but could find no flaw, and the fact that Hughes failed to score, or lay on a goal for a colleague, in 180 minutes of football speaks for itself.

Any continental performer, no matter how talented, might reasonably need a season to become accustomed to the more frenetic demands of the British game, and with this in mind, Glenn Hysen has been a success. If he can build on his solid start, the sight of that distinguished, iron-grey head at the centre of the Reds' rearguard is likely to be a familiar one for several years to come.

BORN: Gothenburg, Sweden, 30.10.59. GAMES: 45. GOALS: 2.
HONOURS: League Championship 89/90. 62 Sweden caps.

OTHER CLUBS: Warta, Sweden; IFK Gothenburg, Sweden (twice); PSV Eindhoven, Holland; Fiorentina, Italy.

## 1989/90 —

KEVIN KEWLEY

KEVIN SHEEDY

STEVE OGRIZOVIC

COLIN RUSSELL

## KEVIN KEWLEY 1977/78

Forward. BORN: Liverpool, 2.3.55. GAMES: 0 (1). GOALS: 0.

## STEVE OGRIZOVIC 1977/78 — 1980/81

Goalkeeper. BORN: Mansfield, 12.9.57. GAMES: 4. GOALS: 0.
OTHER CLUBS: Chesterfield 77/8 (16, 0);
Shrewsbury Town 82/3–83/4 (84, 0);
Coventry City 84/5– (241, 1).

## KEVIN SHEEDY 1980/81 — 1981/82

Midfielder. BORN: Builth Wells, 21.10.59. GAMES: 3 (2).
GOALS: 2. HONOURS: 26 Republic of Ireland caps.
OTHER CLUBS: Hereford United 75/6–77/8 (51, 4);
Everton 82/3– (235, 62).

## COLIN RUSSELL 1980/81

Forward. BORN: Liverpool, 21.1.61. GAMES: 0 (1).
GOALS: 0. OTHER CLUBS: Huddersfield Town 82/3–83/4 (66, 23);
Stoke City *on loan* 83/4 (11, 2); Bournemouth 84/5–85/6 (68, 14);
Doncaster Rovers 86/7–87/8 (43, 5); Scarborough 87/8 (13, 2).

## MARK SEAGRAVES 1985/86

Defender. BORN: Bootle, 22.10.66. GAMES: 2. GOALS: 0.
OTHER CLUBS: Norwich City *on loan* 86/7 (3, 0);
Manchester City 87/8– (42, 0).

## ALAN IRVINE 1986/87 — 1987/88

Forward. BORN: Broxburn, West Lothian, 29.11.62.
GAMES: 0 (4). GOALS: 0. OTHER CLUBS: Falkirk;
Dundee United; Shrewsbury Town 87/8–88/9 (37, 6).

MARK SEAGRAVES

ALAN IRVINE

BRIAN MOONEY

JOHN DURNIN

### BRIAN MOONEY 1986/87

Midfielder. BORN: Dublin, 2.2.66. GAMES: 0 (1).
GOALS: 0. OTHER CLUBS: Home Farm; Wrexham *on loan*
85/6 (9, 2); Preston North End 87/8– (119, 18).

### JOHN DURNIN 1986/87 — 1988/89

Forward. BORN: Liverpool, 18.8.65. GAMES: 1 (1).
GOALS: 0. OTHER CLUBS: West Bromwich Albion *on loan*
88/9 (5, 2); Oxford United 88/9– (61, 16).

### ALEX WATSON 1987/88 —

Central defender. BORN: Liverpool, 6.4.68.
GAMES: 5 (3). GOALS: 0.

### MIKE MARSH 1988/89 —

Forward. BORN: Kirkby, Liverpool, 21.7.69.
GAMES: 0 (3). GOALS: 0.

### NICKY TANNER 1989/90 —

Defender. BORN: Bristol, 24.5.65. GAMES: 2 (2).
GOALS: 0. OTHER CLUBS: Bristol Rovers 85/6–87/8 (107, 3);
Norwich City *on loan* 89/90 (6, 0).

ALEX WATSON

NICKY TANNER

MIKE MARSH

# BILL SHANKLY

Liverpool and Bill Shankly were made for each other. When they joined forces in December 1959, the club was a slumbering mass of unfulfilled potential, the man a soccer boss of only moderate success. But Bill had a vision, and when he set eyes on Anfield he knew he had found the setting for his life's great work. The stadium was a mess and the training ground a wasteland, the team mediocre and the board complacent – but those fans, their spirit and that all-consuming thirst for a football team worthy of the name . . . ah, now they were really something.

The story of Bill's transformation of the Reds has passed into folklore, but what was his secret? How did he do it? Well, to begin with, he was a motivator and psychologist supreme. His players respected him, and some of them might even have feared him a little bit. Eventually, most of them loved him. Above all, no one wanted to let him down. Often outrageous, eternally indomitable, the Ayrshire miner's son built up his men until they felt like giants. Before the 1965 FA Cup Final he told them: 'You are the best. Leeds are honoured to be on the same pitch.' And after watching his side be annihilated 5–1 by Ajax in a 1966 European Cup tie he rasped: 'We've got their measure now. We can still beat them.' Men who played under Bill swear that most of his lurid statements were not made for mere effect; he actually believed them!

Then there was his knowledge of the game. His brain was an encyclopaedia of footballers, their strengths and weaknesses, likes and dislikes – any scrap of information which might one day further the Liverpool cause. His long career as an abrasive wing-half for Carlisle, Preston and Scotland, and his management experience at Carlisle, Grimsby, Workington and Huddersfield inspired his creed for playing the game, which was deceptively simple: 'Get the ball, pass it to the nearest red shirt, and then move into space. It all comes down to give and take.' Bill possessed strong socialist ideals and carried them into his football; the work was shared by everyone in the team and there was no room for prima donnas, though he always resented the description of his side as mechanical, seeing this as an unjust slur.

The Shankly wit, of course, is synonymous with the man, as the Liverpool directors quickly discovered when they asked him if he wanted to take over the best club in the country. 'Why, is Matt Busby packing up?' was his quickfire reply. Having accepted the job, though, Bill knew that he would need more than jokes to resurrect the Reds. He began by retaining the backroom staff; then he set to work on the players. A chosen few stayed, but over the next couple of seasons most of the men who had struggled unavailingly to lift the club out of the Second Division departed. In came the likes of St John and Yeats, and the playing foundations of the most successful soccer dynasty in the history of the British game were laid.

Promotion came in 1961/62 and was swiftly followed by unprecedented glories as the sixties unfolded. The Reds' first FA Cup triumph was sandwiched by two League Championships and there was a series of enthralling European adventures to fire the imagination of the most passionate supporters in the land. Shanks was placed on a pedestal from which not even a barren patch towards the end of the decade could remove him. He went on to build a second fine side and register further triumphs before stunning the soccer world with his retirement – immediately after lifting his second FA Cup – in 1974.

His subsequent relations with the club he had turned into an international institution were tainted with misunderstandings, and perhaps a little more tact might have been exercised on both sides. Bill died of a heart attack in 1981, and the Shankly Gates – inscribed with the legend 'You'll Never Walk Alone' – stand as an appropriate tribute at his beloved Anfield. But his ultimate memorial is something grander, more all-embracing than that – no less than Liverpool FC itself, the club Bill Shankly built.

# MANAGER 1959 — 1974

# BOB PAISLEY

When Bob Paisley moved into the manager's chair unexpectedly vacated by Bill Shankly in the summer of 1974, most pundits saw the modest north-easterner as a two-way loser. If the Reds continued in their winning ways, it would be a case of yet more triumphs for the team that Shanks had created; if, on the other hand, the flow of trophies dried up, then poor old Bob would take the blame. But it didn't happen quite like that.

After one barren campaign, the man who had served Liverpool as player, coach and assistant manager since 1939 began putting his own stamp on the side. Six Championships, three European Cups, one UEFA Cup and three League Cups later, he retired as the most successful boss in English football history. And no one could seriously suggest that his incredible record was the result of anyone's efforts but his own. Of course, Bob would be the first to acknowledge that Bill had laid the foundations, although as number two in the Anfield hierarchy he had undeniably put in some of the spadework himself. With characteristic diffidence, he was reluctant to take the job when it was thrust on him, even urging his predecessor to change his mind about stepping down. In the end, he said he'd do his best . . .

Bob started with the respect of his players, though there may have been traces of resentment in some quarters as a result of tough decisions he had been called on to implement as first lieutenant during the Shankly regime. He probably suffered some early embarrassment, too, when Bill, on appearing at the training ground, was addressed as 'Boss' by some of his former charges. Undaunted, he soldiered on, sensibly deciding not to compete with the wisecracking Scot for the fans' affections. He was no extrovert and had no intention of pretending to be one. 'I'll let the players on the pitch do my talking for me,' he said at the time, and over the seasons that followed their statements were eloquent indeed. To begin with, however, they were not quite so communicative, with no silverware being added to the Anfield collection in 1974/75. The prophets of doom had a field day, predicting that the new manager would prove little more than a caretaker and that some top name was being lined up.

The Paisley way was not to panic. He responded by quietly enhancing his legacy of players, adding the likes of Neal and McDermott to his squad and – a master stroke, this – converting Ray Kennedy from a struggling striker into a vastly influential left-sided midfielder. In 1975/76 he began to enjoy the fruits, with a title and UEFA Cup double to match Bill's identical achievement of three years earlier. Thereafter he began to break new ground, the subsequent campaign yielding the ultimate prize which had perpetually eluded Shanks – the European Cup. As his confidence grew, Bob even began to unbend a little in public, and when asked for his views before that greatest ever British football triumph on Italian soil, he revealed his own brand of wry humour: 'The last time I was in Rome was 33 years ago. I helped to capture it.'

As the honours mounted, the extent of Bob's soccer expertise became ever more apparent. He preached a gospel of control and movement, and made sure that he had the right men to put it into practice, bringing such outstanding talents as Dalglish, Souness and Hansen to the club. A meticulous planner, shrewd tactician and canny judge of a player's strengths and weaknesses, he was also an authority on football injuries, often being able to diagnose problems before they became serious. Refreshingly, he was also willing to own up to his rare mistakes, taking the blame for changing his formation from 4–4–2 to 4–3–3 for the 1979 FA Cup semi-final replay against Manchester United, a switch which he believed cost the Reds the match.

Bob retired in 1983 after nine years in charge, coming back two years later to advise Kenny Dalglish, and eventually taking a seat on the board. Brian Clough said it all when he summed up the Paisley career: 'He is a great man, and has once and for all broken the myth that nice guys don't win anything.'

## MANAGER 1974 — 1983

# JOE FAGAN

Joe Fagan was faced with the seemingly impossible task of following not one, but two legends as boss of the Reds. How did he react? Why, by instantly outdoing them, how else? In his first campaign, Joe achieved what neither Bill Shankly nor Bob Paisley had managed – he led Liverpool to three major honours, the European Cup, the League Championship and the Milk Cup. It was the perfect riposte to critics who had said that not even the all-conquering Anfield outfit could promote from within for a second time and maintain success.

To people who knew the club, though, his triumphs came as no surprise. Joe, whose son Chris made one senior appearance for the Reds in 1971, had been a Liverpool coach since 1958 and had moved up to become Bob's assistant after Bill's retirement. As such, he was imbued with all things Liverpool and was already a vital part of the set-up, albeit a publicly silent one. He had the golden knack of getting the best out of the players in his charge and, in many cases, he was a mixture of friend and adviser to them.

It was from this position of strength that his reign began, inauspiciously as it turned out, with a Charity Shield defeat by Manchester United. But when the real business got under way the status quo of Liverpool dominance was soon restored, and a glorious 1983/84 came to a climax with that nerve-tingling penalty shoot-out to decide the European Cup Final against Roma in Rome. And when Alan Kennedy slotted home the winner, Joe's familiar cheeky grin dominated the celebrations as the enormity of his triple triumph began to sink in.

But there were clouds on the horizon. With his imperious skipper Graeme Souness leaving for Italy, Joe was always going to face a more demanding term in 1984/85, and so it proved. His early years in the game – when he had been an enthusiastic, if moderate performer for Manchester City and Bradford – had taught Joe the virtues of pragmatism, and he declared: 'Souness has gone; forget about him, we've got a job to do without him.' That, however, was easier said than done.

John Wark and Paul Walsh were added to the squad but, partly through injuries, neither player had the hoped-for impact. An appalling League start saw the Reds drop into the bottom three by October, and although they recovered to finish runners-up, the title slipped across Stanley Park to Everton. There was an early Milk Cup exit at the hands of Tottenham, and when progress towards the FA Cup Final was halted by Manchester United in a semi-final replay, all that was left was the European Cup. That Liverpool eventually lost the final to Juventus counted for nothing; that lives were lost when a wall collapsed during crowd trouble at the Heysel Stadium cast a blight over the football world.

Joe, who had already decided to retire, shed tears of despair on that grievous night as he confirmed his decision to step down. So honest, knowledgeable and respected throughout the game, he did not deserve such a dire departure. But despite the trauma of Heysel, Joe Fagan can look back with pride on his two years in charge at Anfield. One former Liverpool star once described him as the top coach in Europe, perhaps the world; another called him a gentleman and a gentle man. Few football managers have left their desks with warmer tributes.

## MANAGER 1983 — 1985

# KENNY DALGLISH

The vultures gathered when Liverpool gave their star performer, Kenny Dalglish, the task of succeeding Joe Fagan as manager. The club had successfully replaced first Bill Shankly and then Bob Paisley by promoting long-time loyal servants, and it was widely expected that yet another graduate from the legendary Anfield bootroom – probably coach Ronnie Moran – would be the man to assume the onerous responsibility. When the job was handed to Kenny, who was to continue as a player, a popular reaction was that, at long last, the board had miscalculated. How could a man with no management experience, and one who was hardly a natural communicator, possibly cope with one of the most demanding positions in football? The Liverpool directors, however, knew a thing or two about Kenny Dalglish. They had perceived the leadership potential and other personal attributes which were to make him worthy of following his illustrious predecessors.

In the early months of the new boss's regime, the doubters began to make smug noises. Ron Atkinson's Manchester United were sweeping all before them and Liverpool were lagging behind. But, come the winter of 1985, United were slipping and, in the spring, Kenny's team blossomed to claim the coveted League and FA Cup double – a feat which had eluded even Messrs Shankly, Paisley and Fagan. The following campaign brought no trophies, but before his reputation could start to slide, Dalglish transformed his side, by means of Barnes and co, into one of the most exciting combinations in Anfield history. Since then the flow of honours has never ceased, and the future could scarcely be more promising.

With the benefit of five years' hindsight, the board's decision to put their faith in Scotland's most-capped footballer takes on the stature of inspiration. Kenny appears to possess a well-nigh ideal cocktail of qualities for a football manager. He is shrewd, single-minded and infinitely knowledgeable about the game; when steel is called for, it's there in abundance; and he is a born winner, as his playing career with both Celtic and the Reds bears impressive witness.

Crucially, Kenny is never afraid to back his judgement, never fearful of leaving favourites such as Beardsley or Rush on the bench. His transfer record is second to none; each of his major signings having integrated effectively into the Liverpool scheme of things. His first acquisition, McMahon, was a brilliant one, and *all* his subsequent expensive investments have proved to be wise, if occasionally of a short-term nature. Arguably an equally important asset is Kenny's absolute refusal to dwell on past triumphs; no matter how swingeing the victory, he usually contends that there should have been more goals, and his after-match comments can invariably be summed up with 'Well, it was nice to win that, but here's to the next one!'

Criticism of his methods seems to leave Kenny cold. When accused of being over-cautious – for putting a sweeper behind two central defenders, for example – he has merely shrugged and turned a deadpan countenance to the world. His relationship with most journalists has been distant; he seems equally untroubled by a good or bad press, and often takes a terse you-saw-it-you-report-it attitude. Humour – albeit of the arid variety – *is* an essential part of the Dalglish persona, though it is usually paraded in public only when he is deflecting some particularly inane media query. Kenny is protective of the club and reacts fiercely to what he considers to be ill-judged comments: former Liverpool player Emlyn Hughes and fellow managers Alex Ferguson and Jim Smith have all fallen foul of his acid tongue.

If his sometimes dismissive statements and reluctance to play the publicity game upsets some people, it certainly doesn't worry Kopites. They don't expect him to be a surrogate Shankly, and respect him not only for his achievements, but also for the dignity and compassion he displayed in the aftermath of the Hillsborough disaster. Kenny Dalglish is a young man, and with so much managerial success already to his credit, it is hard to believe that in the next few years he will not aspire to some new challenge. Any club, or country, which employs him will be guaranteed value for their money.

## PLAYER-MANAGER 1985 –

# PLAYERS' STATISTICS

| Player | Seas | LEAGUE | | | FA CUP | | | L CUP | | | EUROPE | | | TOTAL | | |
|---|---|---|---|---|---|---|---|---|---|---|---|---|---|---|---|---|
| | | Ap | Sb | Gl | Ap | Sb | Gl | Ap | Sb | Gl | Ap | Sb | Gl | Ap | Sb | Gl |
| **Ablett G** | 86- | 67 | (5) | 1 | 11 | (1) | 0 | 7 | (0) | 0 | 0 | | 0 | 85 | (6) | 1 |
| **A'Court A** | 52-64 | 355 | | 61 | 24 | | 2 | 2 | | 0 | 1 | | 0 | 382 | | 63 |
| **Aldridge J** | 86-89 | 69 | (14) | 50 | 12 | | 8 | 7 | (1) | 3 | 0 | | 0 | 88 | (15) | 61 |
| **Arnell A** | 53-60 | 69 | | 33 | 6 | | 2 | 0 | | 0 | 0 | | 0 | 75 | | 35 |
| **Arnold S** | 1970 | 1 | | 0 | 0 | | 0 | 0 | | 0 | 0 | | 0 | 1 | | 0 |
| **Arrowsmith A** | 61-67 | 43 | (4) | 20 | 6 | | 4 | 0 | | 0 | 1 | | 0 | 50 | (4) | 24 |
| **Banks A** | 58-60 | 8 | | 6 | 0 | | 0 | 0 | | 0 | 0 | | 0 | 8 | | 6 |
| **Barnes J** | 87- | 105 | | 45 | 21 | | 10 | 9 | | 3 | 0 | | 0 | 135 | | 58 |
| **Beardsley P** | 87- | 96 | (8) | 35 | 20 | | 9 | 11 | (1) | 1 | 0 | | 0 | 127 | (9) | 45 |
| **Beglin J** | 84-87 | 64 | | 2 | 10 | | 0 | 13 | | 0 | 3 | | 1 | 90 | | 3 |
| **Boersma P** | 69-75 | 73 | (9) | 17 | 7 | (3) | 1 | 5 | (3) | 3 | 13 | (6) | 8 | 98 | (21) | 29 |
| **Brownbill D** | 1973 | 1 | | 0 | 0 | | 0 | 0 | | 0 | 0 | | 0 | 1 | | 0 |
| **Burrows D** | 88- | 39 | (8) | 0 | 5 | (1) | 0 | 3 | | 0 | 0 | | 0 | 47 | (9) | 0 |
| **Byrne G** | 57-68 | 273 | (1) | 2 | 29 | | 0 | 5 | | 0 | 22 | | 1 | 329 | (1) | 3 |
| **Callaghan I** | 59-77 | 637 | (3) | 50 | 77 | (1) | 2 | 42 | | 7 | 87 | (1) | 10 | 843 | (5) | 69 |
| **Campbell R** | 59-60 | 14 | | 1 | 0 | | 0 | 0 | | 0 | 0 | | 0 | 14 | | 1 |
| **Case J** | 74-80 | 170 | (16) | 23 | 20 | (2) | 7 | 21 | (1) | 3 | 25 | (6) | 12 | 236 | (25) | 45 |
| **Chisnall P** | 64-65 | 6 | | 1 | 0 | | 0 | 0 | | 0 | 2 | | 1 | 8 | | 2 |
| **Clemence R** | 68-80 | 470 | | 0 | 54 | | 0 | 55 | | 0 | 77 | | 0 | 656 | | 0 |
| **Cohen A** | 79-80 | 16 | (2) | 1 | 1 | | 0 | 1 | | 0 | 2 | (1) | 0 | 20 | (3) | 1 |
| **Cormack P** | 72-75 | 119 | (6) | 21 | 14 | | 2 | 20 | | 1 | 15 | (3) | 2 | 168 | (9) | 26 |
| **Dalglish K** | 77- | 342 | (16) | 118 | 36 | | 13 | 57 | (2) | 27 | 46 | (1) | 10 | 481 | (16) | 168 |
| **Durnin J** | 86-88 | 0 | | 0 | 0 | | 0 | 1 | (1) | 0 | 0 | | 0 | 1 | (1) | 0 |
| **Evans A** | 68-71 | 77 | (2) | 21 | 9 | (2) | 3 | 7 | | 2 | 11 | (2) | 7 | 104 | (6) | 33 |
| **Evans R** | 69-73 | 9 | | 0 | 0 | | 0 | 1 | | 0 | 1 | | 0 | 11 | | 0 |
| **Fagan C** | 1970 | 1 | | 0 | 0 | | 0 | 0 | | 0 | 0 | | 0 | 1 | | 0 |
| **Fairclough D** | 75-82 | 64 | (36) | 34 | 10 | (4) | 4 | 7 | (13) | 10 | 7 | (9) | 4 | 88 | (62) | 52 |
| **Ferns P** | 62-64 | 27 | | 1 | 1 | | 0 | 0 | | 0 | 0 | | 0 | 28 | | 1 |
| **Furnell J** | 61-63 | 28 | | 0 | 0 | | 0 | 0 | | 0 | 0 | | 0 | 28 | | 0 |
| **Gayle H** | 1980 | 3 | (1) | 1 | 0 | | 0 | 0 | | 0 | 0 | (1) | 0 | 3 | (2) | 1 |
| **Gillespie G** | 83- | 122 | (4) | 13 | 19 | (2) | 0 | 19 | | 1 | 2 | (1) | 0 | 162 | (7) | 14 |
| **Graham R** | 64-71 | 96 | (5) | 31 | 7 | (2) | 4 | 7 | (1) | 2 | 13 | | 5 | 123 | (8) | 42 |
| **Grobbelaar B** | 81- | 338 | | 0 | 44 | | 0 | 56 | | 0 | 30 | | 0 | 468 | | 0 |
| **Hall B** | 68-75 | 140 | (13) | 15 | 17 | (2) | 3 | 12 | (1) | 1 | 27 | (8) | 2 | 196 | (24) | 21 |
| **Hansen A** | 77- | 435 | (2) | 7 | 59 | (1) | 2 | 68 | | 1 | 42 | (1) | 3 | 604 | (4) | 13 |
| **Harrower J** | 57-60 | 96 | | 21 | 6 | | 1 | 3 | | 0 | 0 | | 0 | 105 | | 22 |
| **Hateley A** | 67-68 | 42 | | 17 | 7 | | 8 | 2 | | 0 | 5 | | 3 | 56 | | 28 |
| **Heighway S** | 70-80 | 312 | (17) | 50 | 33 | (3) | 8 | 38 | | 7 | 61 | (3) | 11 | 444 | (23) | 76 |
| **Hickson D** | 59-60 | 60 | | 37 | 4 | | 0 | 3 | | 1 | 0 | | 0 | 67 | | 38 |
| **Hignett A** | 1964 | 1 | | 0 | 0 | | 0 | 0 | | 0 | 0 | | 0 | 1 | | 0 |
| **Hodgson D** | 82-83 | 21 | (7) | 4 | 3 | | 1 | 6 | (3) | 3 | 3 | (4) | 2 | 33 | (14) | 10 |
| **Hooper M** | 86- | 30 | | 0 | 3 | | 0 | 6 | | 0 | 0 | | 0 | 39 | | 0 |
| **Houghton R** | 87- | 80 | (5) | 13 | 15 | (1) | 2 | 8 | | 0 | 0 | | 0 | 103 | (6) | 15 |
| **Hughes E** | 66-78 | 474 | | 35 | 62 | | 1 | 46 | | 3 | 75 | | 9 | 657 | | 48 |
| **Hunt R** | 59-69 | 401 | (3) | 245 | 44 | | 18 | 10 | | 5 | 29 | (2) | 17 | 484 | (5) | 285 |
| **Hysen G** | 89- | 35 | | 1 | 8 | | 0 | 2 | | 1 | 0 | | 0 | 45 | | 2 |
| **Irvine A** | 86-87 | 0 | (2) | 0 | 0 | (1) | 0 | 0 | (1) | 0 | 0 | | 0 | 0 | (4) | 0 |
| **Irwin C** | 79-80 | 26 | (3) | 3 | 4 | | 0 | 6 | | 0 | 4 | (1) | 0 | 40 | (4) | 3 |
| **Johnson D** | 76-81 | 128 | (20) | 55 | 17 | (2) | 6 | 15 | (3) | 9 | 14 | (5) | 8 | 174 | (30) | 78 |
| **Johnston C** | 81-87 | 165 | (25) | 30 | 14 | (4) | 4 | 32 | (3) | 3 | 13 | (4) | 2 | 224 | (36) | 39 |
| **Jones A** | 59-62 | 5 | | 0 | 0 | | 0 | 0 | | 0 | 0 | | 0 | 5 | | 0 |
| **Jones J** | 75-77 | 72 | | 3 | 9 | | 0 | 4 | | 0 | 12 | | 0 | 97 | | 3 |
| **Keegan K** | 71-76 | 230 | | 68 | 28 | | 14 | 23 | | 6 | 40 | | 12 | 321 | | 100 |
| **Kennedy A** | 78-85 | 247 | (2) | 15 | 21 | | 0 | 45 | | 2 | 34 | | 4 | 347 | (2) | 21 |
| **Kennedy R** | 74-81 | 272 | (3) | 51 | 28 | | 3 | 35 | | 6 | 46 | | 12 | 381 | (3) | 72 |
| **Kettle B** | 75-76 | 3 | | 0 | 0 | | 0 | 0 | | 0 | 1 | | 0 | 4 | | 0 |
| **Kewley K** | 1977 | 0 | (1) | 0 | 0 | | 0 | 0 | | 0 | 0 | | 0 | 0 | (1) | 0 |
| **Lane F** | 1972 | 1 | | 0 | 0 | | 0 | 1 | | 0 | 0 | | 0 | 2 | | 0 |
| **Lawler C** | 62-75 | 406 | | 41 | 47 | | 4 | 27 | | 5 | 66 | | 11 | 546 | | 61 |
| **Lawrence T** | 62-70 | 306 | | 0 | 42 | | 0 | 6 | | 0 | 33 | | 0 | 387 | | 0 |
| **Lawrenson M** | 81-87 | 233 | (8) | 11 | 24 | | 2 | 49 | | 2 | 26 | (1) | 2 | 332 | (9) | 17 |
| **Lee S** | 77-85 | 190 | (7) | 13 | 17 | | 0 | 39 | | 2 | 33 | | 4 | 279 | (7) | 19 |
| **Leishman T** | 59-62 | 107 | | 6 | 9 | | 0 | 3 | | 1 | 0 | | 0 | 119 | | 7 |
| **Lewis K** | 60-62 | 71 | | 39 | 8 | | 3 | 2 | | 2 | 0 | | 0 | 81 | | 44 |